THE PUPPY REPORT

THE
PUPPY

AN INDISPENSABLE GUIDE TO

Larry Shook

REPORT

NDING A HEALTHY, LOVABLE DOG

LYONS & BURFORD, PUBLISHERS

Printed in the United States of America

10 9 8 7 6 5 4 3 2

Library of Congress Cataloging-in-Publication Data

Shook, Larry.
    The puppy report : an indispensable guide to finding a healthy, lovable dog / Larry Shook.
        p.   cm.
    ISBN 1-55821-140-3
    1. Dogs.   2. Dogs—Selection.   3. Dog breeds.   4. Dog industry.
    I. Title.
    636.7'0887—dc20   92-12616
                                                                CIP

This book is for my parents from whom I inherited the dog-lover gene, and for Judy, without whose support it couldn't have been written.

Contents

Acknowledgments

I am grateful to Peter Burford for his support in bringing this book into the world and for his skillful editing; to my wife, Judy, for reading and editing the manuscript; to Dr. Herm David for his advice and counsel; to Wayne Cavanaugh of the American Kennel Club for his interview; to Charlene Woodward for introducing me to some of the dog world's most concerned people; to Shannon Hall for all her time and material; to Audrey Dixon of the Canine Eye Registration Foundation; to Dr. E. A. Corley of the Orthopedic Foundation for Animals; to Dr. Richard D. Whipps for all the help he has given me in understanding the ailments of dogs; to Dr. William L. Yakely for helping me understand canine eye disease and for loaning a stranger his copy of the biblical *Inherited Eye Diseases in Purebred Dogs*; to countless members of the canine maquis who helped me along my way.

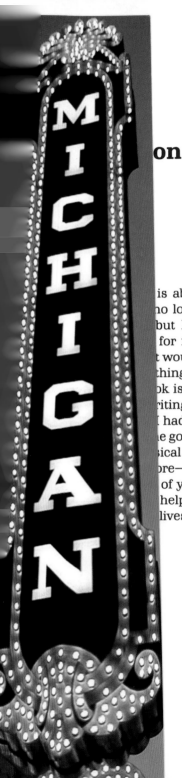

on

is about a crisis now affecting America's
no love them. It may be among the lesser
but I take it seriously because it is bad
for for those of us who like to share life
t would be easier to go without music than
thing friendship of a dog. If you have simi-
ok is for you.

riting it is to help you avoid a painful expe-
I had and find a canine companion who is
e good news is, because of advances in the
sical sciences, it is easier to find a good dog
ore—if you go about it properly. And if you
of yourself and your family in choosing a
helping the nation's dogs and all of us who
lives.

If the door was closed he would wait patiently on the other side, a red ear or paw often protruding beneath the door. That was the Tugger I loved. But there was another Tugger who troubled me right from the start, a Tugger I never understood.

Unlike most puppies, Tugger never had much of a following instinct. For that reason, I soon learned I couldn't take him to parks or open fields when he was small, as I have done with every other puppy I ever owned. Thoroughly independent, the little Terrier would simply take off, and I would eventually have to chase him down. One afternoon when he was only eight weeks old I needed to bring him into the house from the back yard; sometimes he came when called, sometimes not, depending on how busy he was. This time he was thoroughly engaged, so I went to pick him up. The minute I did he was transformed into the cartoon version of a Tasmanian devil, a small red buzz saw, snarling and snapping, utterly outraged by the cheekiness of a man who would so interfere with his affairs. I tried to quiet him, then dominate him. His fury only grew. He drew blood before I could set him down, and I was astounded by the awesome size of this tiny creature's will. I made a mental note to be careful how I handled him lest I turn him into a vicious dog.

The early weeks and months of Tugger's puppyhood were an idyll of charm and play punctuated by his surprising irritability: every now and then he would discipline with a sharp snap one who offended him. Two of my children, nine-year-old Katie and ten-year-old Ben, were both punished in this way for the infraction of hugging the puppy. Neither was permanently scarred, but Ben did get a fat lip from Tugger's facial nip.

"Be sure to get him into a puppy class as soon as he's six months old," advised the breeder. We did, and the whole family participated. Shortly after the first class began the instructor repositioned Tugger and me in the circle of dogs and handlers. I hadn't noticed anything, but she didn't like the way Tugger was eyeing a 120-pound Rottweiler; Tugger weighed all of 30 pounds at the time. When we described Tugger's surliness at home and asked the instructor for advice, she had us stay after so she could evaluate him undistracted by the other pupils.

The instructor didn't like what she saw in Tugger, and no one could blame her. She gave him the sit command. The Terrier defied her by standing, so she popped him expertly with the slip-chain training collar. Tugger countered with a growl. Punishment was instantaneous. Like a Marine drill instructor teaching judo to an unruly recruit, she flipped him on his back, grasped one of his jowls and pinned his head to the floor. This was accompanied by a truly intimidating tongue lashing. The dog was startled, but a bass growl rumbled from his indomitable soul. I imagine Tugger came to regret that as the worst mistake he had yet made. If the trainer had already been tough with our puppy, that was her Mary Poppins act compared to what came next. She slapped Tugger smartly across the muzzle and shook him violently. God only knows what mental images the dog received from the woman, but she must have become the angel of death to him judging from his pathetic cries and yelps. These vocalizations were out of all proportion to any pain he could have felt. The trainer then let him up, spoke sweetly, and told him to sit. He did, gratefully.

"You're really going to have to stay on top of this dog or you could have trouble," the instructor told us. Serious trouble, she meant. The kind where someone gets hurt and a dog winds up with the death penalty. I was all ears. Six months is plenty of time to develop a deep love for an animal you've raised from early puppyhood. At least it is for me. The idea that Tugger might have to be put to sleep for being too aggressive scared and depressed me.

So over the next weeks and months I handled Tugger, or tried to, exactly as I was told. This included daily obedience training with plenty of loving reward, plus instant reprisal, as we had been taught, for any act of surliness. Most of the time Tugger was his good-natured, rocket-spirited self. When the

Mr. Hyde in him did come out in the form of growling at the children or my wife and me for something that didn't suit him, he always submitted to the back treatment and scruff shake—except that he always had to have the last word in the form of a subdued growl. There was no doubt he was cussing us under his breath. At least there was no more biting.

Still, as Tugger grew to maturity, certain troubling behaviors persisted and even escalated. He was too protective of his yard, barking aggressively at passersby. When guests came into the home Tugger made us nervous with his assertive behavior toward them. This was especially perplexing because he had been extensively socialized as a pup, with lots of exposure to visitors on his home ground and plenty of contact with people and animals in the outside world. Eventually Tugger started to jump up on people as they left our house. It was a playful but testing gesture. Each time we would admonish him sternly; it was like water off a boisterous duck's back. Then he started giving little nips, aimed at departing visitors' heels and rumps. The curious thing was that while this was an extremely disconcerting action, it always felt more mischievous than malicious. While Tugger made me nervous, I never thought he would actually try to hurt someone unless he felt he or his family needed protection. Nevertheless, we had to start putting the dog in the kitchen when friends said goodby.

It was at this time a disgusting trait surfaced. When we let Tugger out of the kitchen, he would race to where a visitor had been sitting and lift his leg on the spot. Our howls of protest only made him more discreet in this turf dispute. If one of our children's friends dropped a school backpack in a bedroom, Tugger would urinate on it. When our oldest daughter returned home from college for the summer, Tugger left a puddle in the middle of her beloved feather bed, a high school graduation present. Soon, the terrier was surreptitiously marking various parts of the house for reasons known only to him.

Meanwhile, he seemed less and less trustworthy around small children. Preemptive confinements to kitchen and kennel became regular fixtures of his life. Even so, like an enabler in a relationship with an alcoholic, I was able to focus on the Tugger I loved. Slowly but surely, however, I became the dog's last ally in the family.

Thus, when the event that sealed Tugger's fate happened, it wasn't a complete surprise. I was away on a business trip to Washington, D.C., when I got a call from my wife, Judy. She was badly shaken. So was I by the time she recounted Tugger's crime.

Youngest daughter Katie, eleven by now, was babysitting a two-year-old girl and her five-year-old brother at our house under Judy's supervision. Pizza was served on paper plates, and Judy was helping Katie shepherd the little ones out to the playhouse for their meal. Without provocation and without warning, right before Katie's eyes, Tugger lunged at the little girl—went for *her*, not her pizza. We never knew if he bit her, scratched her, or both, but she received a small cut over her left eye and one on her upper lip. She fell on her back and Tugger stood over her growling viciously, hair on his back standing up. Naturally, the child was screaming in terror, which seemed to incite Tugger even more. Judy dragged him off to his kennel. Fortunately, the little girl's physical injuries were minor, but who knows what kind of emotional trauma lingers after such an experience? Even more distressing was the thought of what might have happened had Judy and Katie not been right there.

Here, then, was a nightmare come true. Countless thoughts raced through my mind, but I knew immediately that it was all over for my dog. He had just turned three years old. "We'll have to put him down," I said.

"Yes," Judy said.

By the time I returned home, though, my resolve to take Tugger's life had collapsed. The idea was simply unbearable. It was barbaric. It was cruel. For all his shortcomings, Tugger loved his family and would have laid down his life unhesitatingly to protect any one of us. Desperately I sought reprieve by consulting local dog experts, breeders, veterinarians. There was consensus: euthanasia was the safest, most responsible thing to do. Sure, there were various training regimens I could try—all of them brutally harsh and very time-consuming—but none of them could assure a successful rehabilitation.

"No matter what you do," a respected local trainer told me, "you will never know for sure that children will be safe with your dog."

Tugger's own breeder, a devoted grandmother who believes in protecting children above all else, was sickened to hear what had happened. Still, she agreed that Tugger should be put to sleep. "I'm glad you're not thinking of trying to find him a 'good home in the country,'" she told me. "That just passes the problem on to someone else. You could never have peace of mind because you could never be sure that he wouldn't someday have contact with another child."

It is against the law to destroy a dog for biting someone, even if he's current on his rabies shots, without first waiting two weeks to confirm the animal's freedom from disease. So Tugger and I spent two weeks on death row together. I knew what was coming. Tugger, the robin chaser, didn't. When I was home, we were together every moment, and when I wasn't there he waited for me in his kennel. I continued to search the literature, like a jailhouse lawyer, for precedent to overturn the verdict. I talked to everyone I knew who knew anything about dogs. Everywhere I turned the advice was the same.

In our last days together I would hug him often, spend long moments sitting in the grass with his head in my lap stroking him, place my cheek against his the better to savor his wonderful dog smell, drink in the living sight of him in great drafts. At first I couldn't cry about losing him. It was like being sick and unable to vomit. I have lost and grieved dogs before. I even once had put to sleep my old dysplastic, arthritic Labrador, Rosie. The day tears came for Tugger I was driving alone in the car. Suddenly my eyes just filled up.

Finally, the day came to take Tugger to the vet for the lethal injection. Judy did it. I didn't have the guts.

Despite everything I have told you, Tugger was for me

mostly sweetness and delight. The trouble is, the rest was darkness, and in that darkness lurked real danger.

The Lessons of Tugger

In more than the obvious way I am responsible for Tugger's death. At the same time, I feel even more guilty about not confronting the reality of his personality earlier. I'm just lucky he didn't maim, or even kill, a child. I still shudder to think how much suffering could have resulted from my carelessness.

Before Tugger's euthanasia I did a great deal of soul-searching, and even more afterwards. What went wrong? What should I have done differently? How could this sad experience have been avoided? Naturally, it is possible to make many more mistakes with a dog than I made with Tugger. But discussions with dog experts, research, and personal reflection reveal that my errors were common and should be shared with others. So here they are in what I consider to be their order of importance.

1. TUGGER'S MOTHER

In hindsight, probably the worst mistake I made with Tugger was getting him in the first place. So antisocial was his mother that when my family first visited the litter the breeder wouldn't let Mama out. She said something about the dam being "uncomfortable with strangers." Finally, we did get to meet the mother—a scared, withdrawn, sullen animal. The breeder was particularly guarded with her around our children. Later, the breeder told me that Tugger's mother was especially hostile toward men. Looking back, I'm amazed I didn't put two and two together. The truth, of course, is that my critical faculties were in neutral at the time. It's what coming under "the spell of puppies" can do to you. After Tugger's death, a veteran breeder of Labrador Retrievers told me that seventy percent of a puppy's personality is inherited from the mother —other breeders put the figure as high as eighty percent. If she is secure, loves people, and knows the world to be good, those are the attitudes she teaches her young. Not all authorities agree that the mother's contribution to temperament is so lopsided. But there is consensus that parent dogs do pass on their personalities, that you should never buy a puppy without seeing at least the mother and, ideally, the father, too. If you don't consider their dispositions suitable for your living arrangement, you shouldn't buy one of their pups.

A little over a year after Tugger was born, his mother went after the breeder's grandson, ripping a leg of his pajamas and narrowly missing the boy's flesh. The breeder had Tugger's mother destroyed. At about the same time one of Tugger's littermates bit a small child in the face, a wound that required stitches. The injured child had merely run up to greet the owner's child at a soccer game. Knowledgeable dog people to whom I have told Tugger's story have a common response. As one put it: "That's a breeding that should never have taken place." What's the old saying about how far an apple falls from the tree?

2. ME

Any dog trainer will tell you that among the worst adversaries of America's dogs are America's dog owners. People ruin dogs in countless ways. In general, however, I believe there are two basic classes of offense: first, misunderstanding of basic dog behavior; and second, failure of dog owners to understand how their own actions toward their pets can confuse them and make them miserable and unstable.

It's really very simple: dogs aren't human. They don't have human brains, they don't have human emotions. It isn't demeaning to dogs to be recognized as *dogs* and treated accordingly. In fact, knowing and honoring a creature's true nature is the sincerest expression of respect.

In my case, I loved Tugger to death—maybe literally. With his strong alpha, or dominant personality, Tugger badly needed to learn psychological and physical boundaries early on. Instead, I fawned over him. I let him jump up on me and sleep on the furniture. Even after attending the puppy class with him for several weeks, it was hard for me to be as consistently firm as I was taught. I wanted to be his pal, not his boss. What I learned—the hard way—is that the *only* way to be a dog's pal *is* to be its boss. It may be that the best dog handler in the world couldn't have made a satisfactory pet of Tugger. It's a cinch, though, that my indulgence didn't help him, or me.

3. THE BREEDER'S ADVICE

Tugger's breeder considered him the pick of the litter because of his appearance. She was happy for me to have him because we lived nearby and she hoped someday to breed him. She warned me, though, that Tugger might well be the most challenging pup in the litter to raise. Observing him with his littermates, I was unable to detect the subtleties of manner that caused her to say that. Moral: experienced breeders develop trained eyes and can be helpful in matching puppies and owners.

4. PUNITIVE TRAINING

Call me superstitious, but I believe a gut feeling shouldn't be ignored. When the instructor of the puppy class used physical intimidation to reprimand Tugger, my gut reaction was not good. It looked, sounded, and felt to me more like abuse than discipline. I understand that thousands of dog handlers all over the world endorse such methods, claiming that millions of well-mannered dogs are proof of their effectiveness. I am not persuaded by this argument and lean toward the theories of positive training discussed in chapter Six. They hold that there is a world of difference between physically dominating a dog into submissive compliance and leading it to good canine citizenship. The former requires only force. The latter necessitates a carefully developed relationship of trust and mutual respect.

Unfortunately, it was too late for Tugger by the time I familiarized myself with these ideas. Since doing so, however, I've realized that not only were the techniques taught in Tugger's puppy class predominantly negative, much of what passes for conventional dog-training wisdom falls into this category. Writer/trainer C. W. Meisterfeld, author of *Jelly Bean versus Dr. Jekyll & Mr. Hyde*, says that the unfortunate results of punitive training methods are made worse by combining them with intermittent overindulgence of the dog. This, of course, was precisely Tugger's learning experience. That realization both angers and saddens me.

TWO

BREEDERS CAN BE HAZARDOUS TO HEALTH

Chief Seattle is supposed to have said that human beings would go crazy without the animals. That sentiment helps explain part of what I feel about Tugger. Anyone who has ever loved a dog knows that if you let the spirit of a dog into your life that spirit lingers long after the animal itself has gone.

I didn't formally decide to get another dog. The threat of doglessness just sets me in motion. Tugger was dead. Gus, a honey-colored Cocker mutt who strayed into our lives during a bitter winter long ago, could go at any time.

So I began the search for a new dog. What I knew for sure was that I *never* wanted another experience like the one I had with Tugger. Canine mortality I can handle. But not capital punishment for dog problems. (This, of course, is a prissy sensitivity for anyone living in a society that executes millions of dogs annually for the crime of becoming unwanted.)

I soon grew irritated and discouraged. I simply could not believe how complicated finding a good dog had become.

Conversations with many dog people and more reading of books that describe breeds (I'd spent an unhurried six months doing such reading before getting Tugger) convinced me that the English Springer Spaniel was a good candidate for my family. By dossier and reputation these dogs love people, are good with kids, are highly trainable, and love a romp in the field. Besides, before Ben and Katie were born I had been an enthusiastic if not very competent bird hunter and had trained a couple of German Shorthaired Pointers and a couple of Labs to the point where they sometimes did what I wanted. I'd often cast an admiring glance toward those doughty little Spaniels with the soulful eyes and happy tails.

But when I began speaking with people who know Springers I was told something I'd never heard before. Stay away from the show lines, the Springer authorities advised, as they are prone to something called Springer rage syndrome. This mysterious, incurable ailment causes dogs to attack without warning. Then another caution: be careful of certain field strains (two of the most celebrated bloodlines were singled out) because they seem unusually susceptible to hereditary blindness.

At this time I hadn't yet learned that getting a dog today is a completely different proposition than it was even a decade ago. I didn't realize that the Humane Society of the United States "conservatively" estimates that one in fifty Americans is bitten by a dog each year. Neither did I know that good dog breeders are a rare, maybe endangered, species themselves; that genetic disease of all kinds is now scourging the nation's dogs like a plague; that America has a canine "Establishment" (imagine) and that it seems to be riddled with moral ambiguity.

Fine, I thought. I'll just treat my search like a reporting assignment. That is how I came to learn the troubling things I am about to tell you.

Naturally, my first goal was to avoid having a dog that would bite. But that, I knew, is a naive goal. Everyone who knows dogs seems to agree that any dog—*any* dog—can be provoked to bite. To help dogs make fight-or-flee decisions rapidly, nature has equipped them with a gas turbine engine of an adrenal system—zero to redline rpm in the blink of an eye. All dogs, of course, are well-armed with teeth. Little dogs conceal derringers in their mouths. Big dogs pack .44 magnums. Why dogs bite is a question for which there isn't a single answer, but down through the long history of canine survival an instinctual adage seems to have been passed along: when in doubt, go with the teeth.

In any event, dogs have been biting people for as long as people have been living with them. After all, "We have chosen to share our homes with carnivores," Humane Society program coordinator Ann Joly told me. "Quite successfully for the most part," she added.

Still, modern dog bite statistics are disturbing and demand attention from everyone who chooses to live with a dog, especially people with children. Aggression is the number one canine behavior problem, according to many animal behavior experts like Dr. Amy Marder, a former professor at the Tufts University School of Veterinary Medicine, now in private practice. Dr. Marder and some of her colleagues can't say for sure if dogs are biting more than they used to, because the studies necessary to make such a determination would be prohibitively expensive.

But even given scientific conservatism, other experts on national dog bite statistics have hunches. "My guess is if we could find the money to do the analysis that would tease out the pertinent data, we would find that both the severity and frequency of dog bites have increased," says Dr. John C. Wright, an associate professor of psychology at Mercer University in Macon, Georgia. Dr. Wright is an animal behaviorist specializing in canine aggression and an officer of the Animal Behavior Society.

In 1989 the number of dog bite fatalities in the U.S. more than doubled to 24, up from 11 the year before, according to the Humane Society. Between 1979 and 1988 the federal Centers for Disease Control (CDC) identified 157 Americans who were killed by dogs. Dr. Jeffrey Sacks, a CDC injury control officer, estimates that the actual number of dog bite fatalities during that period was between 183 and 204. Children under ten accounted for seventy percent of the deaths, according to Dr. Sacks, and 25 infants younger than one year were killed.

The number of people bitten by dogs each year is unclear

because of inadequate reporting. The Humane Society says public health agencies report a million to three million dog bites annually but notes that estimates of unreported bites run between two and forty times higher. "In general, we can conservatively estimate that in a typical year at least one in every 50 Americans is bitten by a dog," Humane Society staffers Guy R. Hodge and Randall Lockwood have written.

Terry Ryan, coordinator of Washington State University's People-Pet Partnership and an internationally recognized authority on canine behavior, says, "By the age of 14 about half of all children have been bitten by a dog."

"There are probably half a million to a million dog bites annually, some terribly disfiguring, requiring medical attention," estimates CDC's Dr. Sacks. The Humane Society's Ann Joly notes that dog bites are one of the leading injuries sending children to the nation's emergency rooms each year. If statistics like these are even partially correct, they portray a national health experience that should satisfy most health care professionals' definition of an epidemic.

In its November 1984 issue, *The Harvard Medical School Health Letter* reported, "A relatively serious and unsolved public health problem is the high frequency with which dogs bite the faces of people, especially children . . . there are some 44,000 *facial* injuries a year from dog bites, and of these 16,000 are severe. Almost all of the worst, and potentially disfiguring, injuries affect children under the age of ten." Most of these bites, said the Harvard publication, are "unprovoked" assaults by family pets.

The cost of better analysis notwithstanding, scientists like CDC's Dr. Sacks are frustrated that steps aren't being taken to quantify the canine aggression problem and isolate causes and solutions. "I can't get people to address the magnitude of the problem," he complains. "You wouldn't believe the occupational hazard dogs now pose to meter readers and mail carriers."

As for dogs and small children, Dr. Sacks has a simple recommendation: don't leave them alone together. The larger the dog and the smaller the child, the more urgent is his advice. "Leaving large dogs and infants alone together is a formula for disaster," he told me. "I love dogs myself, but I've made the decision not to own one until my children are older."

But if scientists and public health officials are hesitant to come out and say that canine aggression is getting worse, at least some of those who work with dogs daily—veterinarians, trainers, animal control officers—aren't.

Since William Campbell began counseling dog owners about the misbehavior of their pets in 1967, he says, he has witnessed the effects of genetic decline on the behavior of dogs "by area, by breeder, and by breed."

"For instance, in the seventies when somebody with an Old English Sheepdog called, our first question was, 'Who has it bitten?' That's how bad Old English Sheepdogs were going," says Campbell, who is author of *Behavior Problems in Dogs* and is one of the nation's most respected dog authorities.

Campbell says when Great Dane owners from Los Angeles contacted him, he asked the same first question: "Who has it bitten?" That was also his first question for callers from "Montana, Kansas, Oregon, Washington, or any of the puppy mill states." (The puppy mill states, found in the Midwest, are discussed later.)

No one should be surprised, says Campbell, that bad breeding can cause bad dispositions. He points out that Doctors John Paul Scott and John L. Fuller, two of the twentieth century's leading canine researchers, long ago documented the role of heredity in canine temperament in their classic *Dog Behavior: The Genetic Basis*.

(Campbell, by the way, based on the experience of his national consulting practice, concludes that aggression is the number six dog behavior problem. Undesirable elimination— pooping and peeing in the house—is number one, he says.)

"As recently as 20 years ago it was predominant in dogs of all breeds not to bite people. That's just not the case anymore," says C. W. Meisterfeld, a professional dog trainer for more than 35 years and author of several dog books. When I spoke with him, he told me of four AKC champion dogs of various breeds from the San Francisco Bay Area that were recently destroyed "because of their sudden vicious Dr. Jekyll and Mr. Hyde behavior."

Meisterfeld cites Swedish police dog training of German Shepherds during the 1930s in which sixty-seven percent of the animals flunked the course because they could not be provoked to bite humans under any circumstance. Today the German Shepherd is ranked as one of the most aggressive breeds by Doctors Benjamin L. Hart and Lynette A. Hart, a husband and wife veterinary/animal behavior team. Their book *The Perfect Puppy* quantifies the behavior of 56 popular dog breeds. (Interestingly, German Shepherds were responsible for fifteen percent of U.S. dog bite fatalities between 1979 and 1988, according to Dr. Sacks, while Pit Bulls and dogs crossed with them caused forty-two percent of the deaths.)

"Canine aggression *has* become an epidemic as far as I can tell," insists a practitioner in one of largest veterinary clinics in my city, Spokane, Washington. He asked me not to use his name. "I've had four-month-old puppies in here that are so aggressive I won't treat them. I also see people keeping such aggressive dogs that I couldn't afford the liability insurance to have them on the premises. Based on what I hear from my colleagues, I'm sure if you polled veterinarians they would report an increase in dog aggression."

"I don't know if we're seeing more total canine aggression, but we're certainly seeing more severe bites. I think it's because people are breeding and keeping more aggressive dogs," says Gail Mackey, executive director of Spokanimal, the animal shelter in my community.

Because the dog is a distillate of the wolf, one of nature's finer predators, more dog bites are probably an unavoidable consequence of bad breeding. "Next to the human, the dog, with about a hundred thousand genes, is the most genetically complex animal on the planet," says Dr. George Padgett, of Michigan State University, and one of the nation's leading canine geneticists. "The dog may be even more genetically complex as far as I know. We have five-pound dogs and 175-pound dogs. You don't find that kind of variation in humans."

The burden of such evidence suggests that when good temperament is not being selected for, generation after generation, it is inevitable that the genetic roulette wheel will stop on aggressive personalities more often than most people would like.

But canine aggression is a complex phenomenon. Dr. Marder, for instance, identifies 12 distinct expressions of it, ranging from dominance to fear to pathophysiology. A behavior gene has not been identified, and no one can say exactly what role breeding plays in a dog's personality, a particular act of aggression, or national dog bite trends. One point of consensus is that a dog's temperament results from the interplay of three factors: heredity, early socialization, and environment. And there is no disagreement that even the descendant of the most kindly parents can be made to bite if the ghost in its blood whispers, "You are in danger."

Given the complexity of the subject, it isn't surprising that many theories about dog bites are now circulating. Here are a few I came across:

• There are no more dog bites today than ever. It's just that as an urban society we're less tolerant of dog bites than we used to be and notice them more.

• As an urban society, we're more stupid about animals than we use to be and unwittingly provoke more dog bites.

• The same two-income family patterns that create latchkey children also create latchkey dogs with the behavior problems that can go along with neglect.

• As society itself has gotten more aggressive, so have society's dogs.

But whatever effect bad breeding is having on the emotional health of dogs, its impact on their physical health is increasingly clear. Talk to dog people and you hear such stories as Sylvia Ellingwood tells.

Like most people who have been involved with purebred dogs for a long time, Ellingwood knows firsthand that dogs have changed dramatically in a remarkably short period. And they are in trouble. Big trouble.

Ellingwood and her husband, Stanley, have been associated with Basset Hounds for 30 years as owners, show ring exhibitors, and field trialers. They competed with the eighth dual champion in the breed's history, and are both AKC-approved field trial judges. Between 1985 and 1990 the Ellingwoods were away from the show circuit. When Ellingwood returned in 1990, as a spectator, she wasn't prepared for what she saw.

"I just couldn't believe the deterioration, not just in Bassets but in a majority of purebreds. A general lack of quality is the best way I can describe it. Bone wasn't there, coats were poor, tails were slinky instead of gay. And lackluster expressions? You looked in the eye of those dogs and something was missing! I talk to other old-timers in the sport and they're as appalled as I am. The thing you have to realize is that dogs aren't like horses that produce only one offspring a year. You can do a lot of damage to dogs in a few short years. And believe me, that damage is being done." She suggested I talk to Carol Veitenheimer about German Shepherds.

A fifty-eight-year-old grandmother, Veitenheimer has loved the German Shepherd dog since she was a girl. As a young woman she began breeding and showing her own Shepherds. The pinnacle of what she calls her "American dogs," was Caji's Fallon. He was a U.S. and Canadian champion and at one time was the seventh-ranked German Shepherd show dog in the land.

Today Veitenheimer makes no bones about her condemnation of those who breed and judge American German Shepherd show dogs. "I continued in the show ring until the German Shepherd breeders got genetically crazy," she says. "They're ruining the breed in this country."

What she means is that German Shepherds now being put up (winning) in the U.S. show ring are caricatures of what the animals once were, or might be again. She says they move peculiarly, are essentially untrainable for any of the things they were originally bred to do, and, although the dogs are glamorous in the eyes of some, they are physical wrecks prone to a wide range of crippling disabilities. And they can be psychological basket cases.

"We're talking about dogs that will run from you howling and hide under a table. Dogs that will cost you a fortune in vet bills," says Veitenheimer.

On two different occasions Veitenheimer bred her top dams to two of the top sires in the country. In both cases the entire litter had to be destroyed because of health problems.

"Every major German Shepherd breeder told me that the main thing is to breed for what wins in the ring." She says in all her experience with owners of champion German Shepherd dogs she only came across one who removed a dog from breeding when she learned it suffered from a hereditary disease (in this case, hip dysplasia, a crippling malady involving badly formed hip joints). "All the others I know breed their champions no matter what's wrong with them."

Ten years ago Veitenheimer had all her American dogs spayed and neutered and placed in homes as pets. She began importing carefully chosen dogs from Germany. Today, she says, her line is physically sound ("ninety-seven percent free of hip dysplasia"), trustworthy with children, and can be trained to do anything German Shepherds were classically bred for. She considers the tastes of the American show ring not only irrelevant but hostile to her breeding program. "I've written judges and told them that as long as they keep putting up the dogs they are, breeders won't change and German Shepherds will keep going downhill."

Already German Shepherds have gone so far downhill there is broad consensus about their poor health. "I would be very, very—*extremely*—cautious about buying a German Shepherd today or recommending that anyone buy one," warns William

Campbell. A main concern about the breed is its high incidence of hip dysplasia. Dr. Dave Prier, head of the pathology department at Washington State University's School of Veterinary Medicine, notes that hip dysplasia was actually "positively selected for" by show breeders of the German Shepherd who like to see a photogenic slope to the haunches of their dogs.

German Shepherds aren't the only breed whose health is in trouble. And hip dysplasia is far from the only worry. John C. Cargill, a longtime breeder of Doberman Pinschers and Akitas, published an article in the January 1991 issue of *Gazette*, official magazine of the American Kennel Club, warning that purebred dogs are now actually in danger of extinction because of genetically transmitted diseases. For this he holds breeders to blame. At the very least, says Campbell, the "genetic bungling" of breeders "may threaten the continued popularity of *Canis familiaris* as a household pet."

Alarmist warnings from a handful of fanatical purists? Read on.

In March 1990, *Atlantic Monthly* magazine fired a national controversy by publishing a cover story called "The Politics of Dogs: How greed and AKC policies are endangering the health and quality of American dogs."

Actually, a cold war had been raging within the nation's dog community for years precisely because of concerns like those expressed here. The physical and behavioral deterioration of what Rudyard Kipling called our "first friends" has grown so pronounced that a virtual chorus of alarm is being raised by people who have devoted their lives to dogs. Because of rampant poor breeding, they suggest that if you go about choosing a dog in such time-honored ways as casually responding to classified ads, going to the local animal shelter, or, heaven forbid, buying from a pet store, you're asking for trouble—heartache at the least, real danger and human tragedy at the worst.

"What are the consequences of not picking a dog carefully today?" asks Susan Bulanda, author of *The Canine Source Book* and a professional trainer for 30 years. She recites a litany of possible miseries. (1) "A bad dog that bites someone. You could wind up with a lawsuit, lose your home, have your salary attached." (2) "A dog with genetic defects. I have a client who didn't do her homework who told me that in the year she's had her dog it's cost her $2,000 in veterinary bills." (3) "A dog that's just not suited for you. Then you're going to somebody like me to try to straighten it out because the kids love the dog, you love the dog, and you can't part with the dog, but the dog's messing your life up. It's not a joy, it's not a pleasure, it's not something you want to live with."

Throughout the Kitsap Peninsula of Washington State, Shannon Hall enjoys a solid reputation as a dog trainer. Vets in the region refer their clients to her. If you are writing a book about how to find a good dog, pillars of the dog community in nearby Seattle will send you to Hall. A dog trainer for two-and-a-half decades, she is considered a reliable authority on what ails dogs most. In her opinion, the biggest problem is dog breeders. "I'm disgusted with breeders," she says.

Hall's own favorite breed is the Collie,[1] but she won't recommend you buy one today. "I'm telling people to just stay away from Collies unless they're prepared to risk the heartbreak and veterinary expense," she says, voicing a caution born of her own painful experience. In the last six years she has owned eight Collies, and not one has been healthy.

She had to destroy one puppy at 18 months, on the recommendation of veterinarians, because "behavioral seizures" were causing it to try to kill other dogs. A four-year-old Collie of hers had to be put down because of constant pain from untreatable spinal problems. A Collie mix she rescued from a shelter (half Collie, quarter German Shepherd, quarter Golden Retriever) suffered simultaneously from hereditary diseases common to all three breeds: hip dysplasia, hypothyroidism, and pancreatitis. That dog's pancreatitis got so bad Hall had to have it

---

[1]By which reference I mean the Scotch, or Lassie-type, collie.

put down at age six. As this book went to press Shannon was nursing a three-year-old Collie that had already cost more than $3,000 in veterinary bills because of back problems, muscle problems, and food and drug allergies. (This particular dog is "behaviorally great," but has to be lifted in and out of Hall's car. His food is specially ordered from Oregon because he can't tolerate anything else.) Hall's tri-color Collie is physically sound but an emotional mess. That's because he spent most of his first five months in a crate. His breeder was a district director of the Collie Club of America who Hall says kept 40 dogs in her living room in crates. Hall took the dog because she felt sorry for him. "He's done more damage to my house than any dog we've ever owned," she says. Hall's sixteen-month-old Collie puppy has been diagnosed by four different vets as having a mysterious and untreatable spinal problem. He is currently undergoing weekly acupuncture at 20 dollars per session. Still another of her Collies is also handicapped by back problems.

"Collies are supposed to live to be fourteen," Hall laments, "but I've only kept one alive past six, a rescued dog, and she is going blind."

Hall is bitter about the well-known Collie breeder in her area, also a member of the Collie Club of America, who offered to sell her a puppy which the breeder admitted was a carrier of progressive retinal atrophy, a blinding hereditary eye disease. Even worse, says Hall, is that it wasn't a test breeding that produced the puppy. In other words, the breeder intentionally mated dogs which she knew to be afflicted with the devastating eye disease.

Hall stresses that Collies are by no means the only genetically ailing breed she sees. "In all breeds I deal with there are major hereditary health problems today."

So every day she finds herself ministering to dog owners who have unwillingly become nurses to the halt and the lame and the emotionally unstable. She tells of young Rottweilers so infirm with hereditary bone disease that they have trouble going up and down stairs and can't be trained for obedience work. She knows of Great Pyrenees kennels breeding dogs too aggressive to live with. One of her clients has a year-old Cocker who is already going blind from cataracts and tests borderline for a bleeding disorder known as von Willebrand's disease. The breeder who sold the woman the Cocker made her sign an agreement not to neuter the dog because she wants to breed from it. Despite its now-known affliction with hereditary illness, the breeder still may want to breed to it.

Because of experiences like these, Hall says, "I can't define 'reputable breeder.' I'm not trying to be snotty, but I don't know what reputable breeder means, because I see the very ones who claim to be [reputable] engaging in these kinds of practices. I don't trust any breeders anymore. I'm in the profession of dogs, and all I can say to my clients is 'buyer beware.' I don't have a list of breeders I will refer to."

On the other side of the continent, Robin Kovary, a professional dog trainer in New York City, shares Hall's concerns. "I see a handful of terrific breeders doing their absolute best to make things better," she told me. But haphazard, irresponsible breeding in the U.S. has become the rule rather than the exception, she believes. "I would have a moral problem with referring people to breeders I didn't know extremely well. You have to do your own research and make your own decisions" about where to get a puppy, she insists.

Kovary is especially distressed by the "severe temperament problems and phobic reactions" she sees among many dogs. She even named two breeds—increasingly popular ones— about which she has particular concern unless the puppies receive extensive socialization to compensate for what appears to be a hereditary tendency toward phobias. But she wouldn't let me quote her naming these breeds for fear of the backlash.

"We are in serious trouble," says Dr. W. Jean Dodds, one of America's top canine scientists. "And there is no question that all of the diseases we're studying today are much more common than they were." A veterinarian specializing in genetic disease, Dr. Dodds regularly speaks out on the subject in her column in *DVM, The Newsmagazine of Veterinary Medicine.* "The biggest problem is a people problem," she told me. "Until the critical mass of conscientious dog breeders becomes more than a minority, you're still going to have people who are more concerned about the self-gratification of ego from producing a beautiful animal and winning awards that translate into the sale of puppies and prestige." Until breeders recognize their ethical responsibility, she says, genetic disease will continue to plague dogs.

The good news, most dog people agree, is that the people problem Dr. Dodds refers to is infinitely solvable. Breeders can do their homework and breed genetically sound dogs. Buyers can do their homework and seek out breeders who care about producing healthy dogs. Both parties can take these actions if they want to.

The bad news: at the moment these are the two biggest "ifs" in dogdom.

While no one would prefer a genetically sick dog over a genetically sound one, the evidence suggests that many members of today's competitive dog tribes would rather breed and own sick winners than healthy losers. Otherwise, why wouldn't the majority of those who show and trial dogs insist their animals be clear of genetic disease before breeding them? Why wouldn't their organizations—breed clubs, field trial associations, AKC itself—require genetic health as a condition of competition or at least of registered procreation?

Michigan State's George Padgett has made the point that even with the current prevalence of genetic disease, if breeders could be persuaded to freely share information about known genetic defects harbored by their bloodlines, if they could be prevailed upon to cooperate fully with one another in weeding out these ailments, most breeds could be substantially rid of their worst hereditary afflictions in about ten years.

But right now that kind of cooperation is only a dream. Dr.

Ian Dunbar, a veterinarian, animal behaviorist, and creator of the well-regarded Sirius Puppy Training Program, has written in AKC's *Gazette* that when breed clubs try to regulate and enforce good breeding practices, their efforts usually end up in back-stabbing. When Dr. R. F. Greathouse, the Collie Club of America's health policy committee chairman, admonished his fellow breeders for the "great many problems with the health and genetic makeup of our Collies," he called on them to accept recommended changes in breeding practices based on "irrefutable" findings that Collies have become a sickly lot. Wrote Dr. Greathouse: "If [breeders] continue to ignore these recommendations—as they obviously have for the past 25 years—then our breed is still going to be in a mess of trouble."

It takes skill to breed good dogs. Correcting genetic pestilence in whole breeds requires more than skill. It needs communal will, because dog breeds reflect shared vision. Such an expression of popular will in the nation's dog culture seems unlikely unless the culture itself changes. Chris Walkowicz, a breeder since 1970 and author of the *Atlas of Dog Breeds*, agrees with Dr. Dodds in suggesting that what is really needed is an elevation in the ethics of dogdom. In the "Breeders Forum" column of AKC *Gazette* she wrote that until breeders start being honest about the widespread ailments resulting from currently accepted breeding practices, breeders must share the blame for "destroying" purebred dogs. Walkowicz applauds the two German Shorthaired Pointer owners and two owners of top-winning Cockers who acknowledged in their breed publications that their dogs were being retired from breeding and competition because genetic defects were discovered in them —hip dysplasia in the case of the Shorthairs, eye problems in the Cockers. She suggests that breeders like these should be role models for those interested in rebuilding the health of purebred dogs.

Such pleas and acts of candor are starting to have an impact on the dog world's mainstream culture. Still, the undertow of that culture, says trainer and Collie lover Shannon Hall, remains strong. As evidence she cites the official breeding recommendations of the Collie Club of America, set out in *The New Collie*. There Collie breeders are urged to breed young males as soon as they become sexually competent, between nine and fifteen months. The same recommendation is made in *The Collie: A Veterinary Reference for the Professional Breeder*, by Dr. Sharon Lynn Vanderlip, a veterinarian. She stresses the importance of using stud Collies at the earliest possible date, "ideally" when the dogs are nine to ten months of age. The problem with that advice is that many genetic ailments appear only with maturity—certain organ problems, for instance, like pancreatitis, or skeletal maladies like spondylosis, in which vertebra collapse, or hip dysplasia. Dogs can't even be X-rayed for clearance of hip dysplasia (discussed in chapter Four) by the Orthopedic Foundation for Animals (OFA) until they are twenty-four months old. Many sources I interviewed, and whose work I came across, took strong exception to the advice to breed such young dogs. Dr. John Kramer, a pathologist at the Washington State University School of Veterinary Medicine, Dr. Dodds, and William Campbell all staunchly oppose the practice. Dr. Carmelo Battaglia, author of *Breeding Better Dogs*, told me, "Be very impressed when you see older dogs" in a breeding program. Ian Dunbar recommends not breeding males until they are five to seven years old or females until the age of three. In this way longevity and sound general health can be selected for.

A major problem of concern to breeders today, even the most dedicated and ethical ones, is what scientists call "data gaps." The data gaps surrounding genetic disease in dogs are cavernous because funding has not been available to compile a comprehensive index of the ailments as they affect the various breeds. Still, for breeders committed to act, remedies are available. One is simply to avail themselves of the existing technology, using "biochemical markers" that Dr. Dodds refers to (see chapter Four) and *never* breed in ways tolerant of genetic disease.

As a puppy buyer, however, you need to understand how hard it can be for dog breeders to follow this seemingly simple recommendation. One of the most caring, expert, and highly respected sources I spoke to, an AKC judge and, for the most part, an AKC advocate, told me a story that puts the issue in perspective. She once owned a champion German Shepherd female, a magnificent animal who exemplified her breed. As the dog was piling up wins in the obedience ring it occurred to the woman that she might have the animal's hips checked. Not because there was a problem with movement, but just to insure soundness. "I decided not to have her X-rayed," the woman told me. "If she was dysplastic I didn't want to know." After the dog became an obedience champion she was X-rayed. Verdict: dysplastic. (I didn't ask if the dog was ever bred.)

Even without turning to the wonders of molecular science, however, breeders can breed healthy dogs. One way is to follow the procedures set out in Carmelo Battaglia's *Breeding Better Dogs*. Battaglia developed his methods while working under a large Navy grant on animal breeding projects as part of his graduate work in psychology. His methods include the use of both a color chart and a symbols chart to visualize the conformation, health, and temperament characteristics of prospective parent dogs and their siblings. Impressive results have been reported from the Battaglia method.

What needs to be emphasized is that breeding experts like Dr. Battaglia stress that just because a dog carries defective genes is not necessarily a reason for removing it from a breeding program. If a dog is outstanding in other respects, it is often possible to breed it in ways that pass its genetic virtues through while filtering out its genetic faults. Battaglia told me that the most dysplastic dog he ever saw appeared to be a phenomenal animal in every other respect and possessed every title but an OFA number (see chapter Four). The X-rays showed the dog "had no hip sockets. None. There were just none there." Battaglia says the average breeder should never breed such an animal, but he might have, assuming close scrutiny convinced him that the dog's other traits were strong enough to justify it. Why? Because "there's an awful lot of research that says if the littermates of the dog you want to breed have good hips and if the parents have good hips, bred to almost anything it will produce good hips. The question is, is it a great dog you want to breed? Is it worth taking the risk? Because if you're wrong you could produce puppies that are going to be sold to people who are going to have heartbreaks down the road."

In the cause of breed improvement, a certain amount of this type of breeding is essential since genetic purity does not exist in nature. Research shows that just as every human carries anywhere from three to five significantly defective genes, the same is true of dogs. Most dog breeds are thought to average around 14 defective genes which must constantly be selected against or balanced in breeding. Just as a skewed approach to breeding can produce glamorous invalids, so can it produce dogs with great hips but weak hearts, or with solid physiques, sound health, and brilliant working instincts but slightly inturned eyelids needing minor surgical correction.

Dr. Padgett cautions against seeing dogs in unrealistically ideal terms. "We try to think about dogs like they can be perfect," he says. "But when we see someone wearing glasses walking down the street we don't say to ourselves, 'There goes someone with genetic disease.'"

The important thing, says Padgett, is the core values which guide the bulk of dog breeding. "Right now by far the largest breeder pool in the country is in conformation [i.e., AKC dog show standards]. Twenty years from now you'll see more emphasis on performance." This is so, he says, because breeders' current values are catching up with them. "I believe if you don't actively select against a problem it can drift in."

Dr. Kramer tells a story about field trial Labrador Retrievers that underscores Dr. Padgett's point. Ironically, it reveals how obsession with performance can be every bit as devastating to canine health as obsession with appearance. Thirty years ago, says Kramer, a bizarre inherited Type 2 muscle fiber deficiency disease was introduced to American Labradors by a single imported stud. He became a great champion and the top stud in the country. "Everybody bred to him," says Kramer, and soon the disease was "fairly well distributed throughout this country. Before you knew it we had a real problem that could be traced back to that dog." The disease, which "continues to be spread today but it's not readily diagnosed," results in lameness by causing deficiency in roughly half of the dog's muscle fibers. It usually doesn't show up until a dog is about six months old. Fortunately, this particular disease has proved to be somewhat self-limiting, because dogs suffering from it, as opposed to those merely carrying the genes, are often unable to breed.

THREE

The Dog Tribes

In looking for a good dog, it's the most natural thing in the world to seek expert guidance. Today it's also absolutely essential. Just don't expect consensus. In fact, gird your loins, for you are about to enter a briar patch of opinion. Feelings about dogs border on religious fervor. Challenge someone's dog values and you're messing with the meaning of life. "Get two Border Collie people in the same room," writer Donald McCaig told me, "and you've got two different opinions."

McCaig is actually talking about Border Collie People, two members of the same tribe. They need to be understood the same way Oglala and Hunkpapa Sioux are understood, Shiite and Sunnite Moslems, Yankees and Southerners, Republicans and Democrats—Democrats and Democrats for that matter. Just imagine the gulfs than can exist among, say, Show Dog People, or between Show Dog People and Field Trial People, or between both of those tribes and Pet Dog People, or Animal Shelter People and Dog Breeder People.

A major reason I settled on getting an Irish Terrier was the good press the dogs get in virtually every breed book you'll ever read.

"Playful with children and a zealous family guardian."— *Man's Best Friend*, National Geographic Book of Dogs, Revised Edition.

"Fine for novice owners. . . . Good with children . . . a gallant gentleman. . . . He can adapt to any home."—*Your Purebred Puppy: A Buyer's Guide*, by Michele Lowell.

"Irish Terriers are excellent family dogs. . . . They are extremely affectionate and gravitate to children . . . lively and full of fun."— *Medical and Genetic Aspects of Purebred Dogs*, by Ross D. Clark, DVM and Joan R. Stainer.

After Tugger's demise, when I was trying to make sense of his short life, individuals with considerably more dog expertise than I had other advice to give:

"I shudder anytime a family with kids decides to get a terrier of any breed."—Shelly Monroe, dog trainer and breeder of Soft-Coated Wheaten Terriers.

"Had you read up carefully on terriers and on Irish Terriers in particular, you may have prudently decided that this was not a breed for your home. . . . If you want another dog I suggest you get one of the sporting breeds, or my first choice, a carefully selected Poodle. The Poodle more than any other breed wraps up in one package most of the things a family wants in a dog."—Robert S. Walker, AKC-approved judge for 21 breeds, retired Cocker Spaniel breeder.

"I wouldn't have an Irish Terrier. They're much too aggressive with other dogs."—Cherie Graves, longtime breeder of American Staffordshire Terriers, and president, Responsible Dog Owners of The Western States.

Still, there were also those who agreed with the books.

"When you told me you had an Irish Terrier I said to myself, 'There's a classy guy.' I've always thought that if I was going to get a terrier, an Irish is the kind I'd get."—Terry Ryan, People-Pet Partnership coordinator, Washington State University, and past president, National Association of Dog Obedience Instructors.

"A well-bred Irish is an excellent dog for a family with children. Nothing will stand between Irish and their families. They're known for going to any lengths to protect them. Irish Terriers, especially males, can be aggressive with other dogs, but they should never be aggressive with people. When you see Irish around children it's like they become one with the children. It's almost as though it's bred into them to join with children's spirits. I've never known anyone with a good Irish not to remark on it.

"Ellis West, a former president of our national breed club, says he won't sell an Irish to a family without children if he can help it. When we lived in San Francisco our Finn would run up to baby carriages in Golden Gate Park. He'd stand up on his hind legs to look in, and when he saw the baby his whole body would become one wiggle. Once Finn and I were walking across the street from a post office in Alameda. A three-year-old was throwing a tantrum in the parking lot and the mother gave her a swat on the bottom and told her to get in the car. Before I knew what was happening Finn whirled around, dashed across the street and stood between the mother and the baby like a statue. He didn't make a sound. When I got there the baby was holding onto Finn's back. 'Oh, my,' said the woman. 'What'd I do?' 'You made the baby cry,' I said. That family got an Irish Terrier."—Mary O'Brien, president, Irish Terrier Club of Northern California, and director, Irish Terrier Club of America.

As you will discover when you begin talking to breeders, some of the most bitter rivalries exist within the breed clubs themselves. They have to do with the basic breed characteristics that should be selected for, as well as infinite "political" disputes. The latter, as nearly as I can tell, have no more relevance to the average dog owner than astronomers' arguments over the "big-bang" theory of the universe.

Outside dogdom's inner circle, though, points of the debate are less fine. For one thing, public revulsion is mounting toward the scandalous, ongoing dumping of unwanted dogs in the nation's animal shelters. One "responsible dog owner" I met wrote an opinion piece entitled "The 'Pet Overpopulation' Hoax," arguing, as you might surmise, that pet overpopulation is just one more invention of a sensation-hungry media.

Call it what you want. In San Mateo, California, the county

board of supervisors woke up, smelled the coffee down at the Peninsula Humane Society, and passed America's first no-breeding ordinance. It requires that dog and cat owners either have their pets sterilized or buy a costly breeder's license. The law has already spawned similar edicts around the country.

Too, media accounts of dog attacks are fueling a growing anti-dog sentiment. "Breed-specific laws" are being proposed around the country to ban the types of dogs considered dangerous. Targeted breeds have included not only Pit Bulls, Rottweilers and German Shepherds, but Golden Retrievers, Labrador Retrievers, English Springer Spaniels, and even mixed breeds. Meanwhile, extreme groups like People for the Ethical Treatment of Animals (PETA) call for the end not only of pet dogs but of all animal domestication. Even dog supporters, however, are alarmed by the incidence of dog attacks. "When I look at pictures of children who have been consumed by dogs I sometimes wonder why we have dogs," the Humane Society's Ann Joly told me.

But what is probably the pivotal dog battle in the country has been going on longer than the shooting in Lebanon. It revolves around the argument over whether dogs should be bred to embrace a balance of traits or a handful of arbitrary beauty features and performance capabilities.

There are various camps in the clash of the dog tribes. Those who endorse the golden mean of functional, temperamentally and physically sound dogs argue that we should be guided by tradition. The dog, they point out, was distilled by intentional breeding to be a companion of, and perform various services for, humanity. It would be a shame to lose this old friend now to fashion, compulsion, or indifference. Some show breeders (not all) insist on their right to produce dogs that catch a judge's eye, never mind whether the animals are good with people, possess the wits to do a lick of work, need cosmetic surgery to be glamorous, or carry within them the seeds of genetic ruin.

A similar obsession applies to some (not all) field trialers whose dogs rarely have human interaction except during training and competition. It's an undeniable fact that many field trial dogs are too high-strung to make even decent hunting companions, much less companions of the hearth. Field trial Labrador Retrievers are an example. Old-timers of retriever trialing express dismay that many of today's top Labs are untrainable without the use of electronic shock collars and other harsh methods.

The point is, there are extremists in both show and field camps who view their dogs not as feeling creatures but as sporting goods. And then there are the puppy farmers. To them, dogs are a crop. These traffickers resist outside interference by watchdog groups like the Humane Society much as some industrial polluters shun environmental protection.

In the eye of this storm you'll find the American Kennel Club. Like bad breath in dogs, controversy has hung over the nation's largest canine registry for a long time now. Today AKC is hounded by an army of critics. Many of those critics constitute a dedicated resistance to AKC policies; they are the maquis of the dog tribes. They consider AKC an active threat to the welfare of dogs and dog owners.

Naturally, AKC and its defenders see things differently. They point out that the organization funds important canine research and sanctions dog events of all kinds that bring joy to the lives of many thousands of people annually.

Inevitably, the truth about the American Kennel Club—the extent to which it does well by dogs and their owners, how far it might fall short—lies somewhere in between the accusations and rebuttals. I make no pretense at resolving the matter, nor to even having tried. My purpose in summarizing the controversy here is to make a simple point: for the average person on a quest for a good dog, AKC registration means very little. In fact, a California law passed in 1991 says as much. It requires pet stores to hang a sign on their cages with this disclaimer:

Breed or pedigree registration does not ensure a healthy dog, nor does it guarantee the quality of the breeding conditions of a dog or the quality of a dog.

In a sense the California law—passed by the nation's social trend-setting state—is an indictment of the dominant culture within AKC which has accepted the progressive crippling of dogs in the cause of making them showier.

The California law should shock no one at AKC. There is a now-famous exchange in which former AKC president William F. Stifel was asked what the organization's response would be to someone who wanted to register a blind, deaf, dysplastic, three-legged purebred puppy with green fur. "We would register the dog," *Parade* magazine quoted Stifel as saying, "AKC unfortunately does not mean quality."

A partial AKC rap sheet looks like this.

THE CLIQUE

AKC supporters refer to the club as a democratic organization. Critics counter that it has repeatedly exhibited despotic tendencies. The most recently cited example is the mysterious case of the Australian Shepherd, which was subjected to what some have called a hostile takeover by AKC in the spring of 1991. This herding dog belonged to the largest independent breed club in America outside AKC—4,000 members, 60,000 dogs registered since 1957. Fearing AKC's record of contributing to the ruin of canine genetics, members of the Australian Shepherd Club of America (ASCA) had steadfastly resisted AKC's embrace. In 1985, the last time its members voted on whether to accept AKC recognition (and thus subject ASCA stock dogs to show dog breeding standards), by a vote of more than two to one the electorate said no thanks. Yet in April 1991 a mystery group calling itself the Australian Shepherd Association petitioned AKC for recognition. "No one in our fancy ever heard of this ASA and still don't know who they are," complained the ASCA board of directors in a letter to its members and the public. It didn't matter, though. AKC told the 4,000 members of the old club that they could either go along with the move by merging with the 133 unknown members of the new club, or have the new organization become the breed's top dog in the eyes of AKC. That would give the newcomers exclusive authority to draft show dog standards. At this writing, the Australian Shepherd appears to have been effectively annexed by AKC. Ethel Conrad, president of the United States Border Collie Club, prefers another interpretation. "The AKC raped the Aussie," she says.

Whatever you call it, the action sent tremors through the U.S. dog community. "I was appalled when the AKC instituted what can only be described as a 'hostile takeover' of your lovely breed," Pam Burkley wrote the ASCA board of directors. Burkley is a longtime breeder of Cavalier King Charles Spaniels and an active member of her breed's club. "I want you to know the eyes of the ENTIRE dog world are on you. . . . Naturally, our members are worried it will happen to our Cavaliers. . . . regardless of what happens, our National Club will stand and we will not turn over our stud book and apply for [AKC] recognition. However, ASCA will set precedence. What happens to you will be the future of most of the nonrecognized breeds." Burkley urged the Aussie lovers to fight. "Hold your ground, folks, just hold your ground!" she wrote. To me she confided, "AKC certainly doesn't care about how it looks to the rest of the world. They don't care what people think about them. They're just wrapped up in getting that registration money."

Critics charge that the episode represents vintage AKC tactics. "Arrogant and authoritarian" is how Border Collie owner Donald McCaig describes AKC's usual way of dealing with the dog public. He tells of a clinic in which AKC representatives were describing the club's new herding trial program. Naturally, the audience was full of questions. "I was stunned," says McCaig. "They were supposed to be teaching people about the new program, but every time someone would ask, 'Why are you doing it this way? It doesn't make any sense,' the AKC reps just would smile and say, 'Because we're doing it that way.' That was the *end* of it. No more discussion. 'If we decide to do it another way, we'll do it another way.' I mean, holy Toledo!"

AKC's adversaries also complain about the organization's secrecy; its bylaws ban reporters from the delegate meetings in which policies are discussed. Critics also contend that AKC is inordinately influenced by two of the country's oldest and wealthiest dog societies, the Westminster and Westchester kennel clubs of New York. Both clubs are male-only organizations. Each consists of fewer than a 100 members, whose well-heeled circumstances may put them out of touch with the concerns of most American dog owners.

SKIN DEEP BEAUTY

The standards by which dogs are judged in the AKC show ring are "beauty manuals only," as American Staffordshire Terrier breeder Cherie Graves puts it. This preoccupation with skin-deep beauty may produce fleeting glory in the show ring and impulse purchases at the pet store. But its shortsightedness has brought genetic mutilation to countless breeds like the Cocker Spaniel and Irish Setter. Cockers used to be known as "merry hunters" and were famous for gentleness with children and devotion to family. Unfortunately, the little spaniels were also cute. Today, because of myopic breeding, Cockers are still cute—show Cockers are even glamorous—but are as out of place in the field as a mink coat in a duck blind. Their formerly sweet nature has been overtaken by a notoriously unpleasant temperament. ("Cockers are considered the number one biter in the nation," says Washington State University's Terry Ryan.)

As for the Irish Setter, it was once legendary for its birdiness. Today it is a legend for being birdbrained. Dual champions

—field and show—among America's sporting dogs are now the next thing to extinct because the dogs' genetic inheritance has been plundered by obsessively competitive and heartlessly commercial breeding. Among the most responsible parties are dilettante show breeders—who stay with the sport just long enough to win a ribbon or two—and puppy farmers. Many sources I spoke with, from veterinary researchers to active show participants, complain that most newcomers to dog showing stay with it for an average of only five years. Puppy farmers breed the dogs that momentarily sell best— Akitas, Shar-Peis, whatever. The time frames in both cases are sufficient to stroke one's ego, make a quick buck, and lay waste to canine gene pools decades and even centuries old.

FETISHES AND MUTILATION

So extreme has been AKC's preoccupation with the appearance of dogs that you might consider it a fetish. Particularly since it has been accompanied by marked deterioration in physical health and temperament. To again use the unfortunate Collie as an example, Washington State University veterinary pathology department chairman Dave Prier points out that show Collie breeders "selected for a head that showed no stop at the eyes. Smaller and smaller eyes were selected for, and that's one reason why Collies have so many eye problems today."

What is even more macabre is the willingness of some show people to turn to the knife if breeding fails to produce winning looks. Other show people deplore and even combat this practice. But given AKC's cultural bias toward looking good over actually being good, it isn't surprising that cosmetic surgery is a reality in the show ring, even though it is grounds for disqualification if detected.

Dog World magazine special features editor Dr. Herm David has written many times about incidents of cosmetic surgery.

In the magazine's July 1991 issue, for instance, he reported on ugly allegations of the practice being carried out by a professional handler on dog show grounds—no anesthesia, no antiseptics. David wrote that AKC gave a flimsy excuse for not investigating the matter, and he raised the possibility of an AKC coverup. Another case David has written of involved an Airedale Terrier that had its tail carriage doctored by a handler at the prestigious Westchester show in 1989. The handler couldn't stop the bleeding; the dog died in the night; the attending vet filed a complaint against the handler with New York State. Charge: unlicensed practice. AKC, says David, suspended the handler for three months.

AKC's critics note the irony that a dog would be banned from the show ring for life for having cosmetic surgery done on it (assuming it survived the procedure) while the "surgeon" would be welcomed back to the fold after just three months. (As we will soon explore, the AKC says a six-month suspension was handed out.)

PUPPY MILLS

For at least four decades puppy mills have been one of the most shameful embarrassments of the dog world. Many AKC critics are particularly incensed that the organization hasn't done more to attack the problem, arguably one of the most cruel and pervasive examples of animal abuse in the nation's history. By Humane Society estimates, puppy mills are almost the exclusive suppliers of the approximately half-million puppies sold annually through America's pet stores. There are an estimated 5000 puppy mills in the country. They are concentrated mostly in six midwestern states—Kansas, Missouri, Nebraska, Iowa, Oklahoma, and Arkansas—referred to as "the puppy mill archipelago" by the American Society for the Prevention of Cruelty to Animals (ASPCA). California is cracking down on puppy mills. Kansas, on the other hand, has made it a felony to sneak into a puppy mill and photograph or otherwise document its activities.

Pet store operators will tell you *their* dogs don't come from puppy mills. The ASPCA estimates that only about ten percent of all pet store dogs are non-puppy-mill animals. Numerous investigations have documented the often barbaric conditions of these operations. Puppy mill dogs are found being raised on wire, like chickens, or in cramped quarters, like veal. Dams and sires live their entire lives in cages and are bred nonstop from the time they are six months old until five or six years of age. When females have mothered themselves to exhaustion and their litter sizes drop, they are often killed. ASPCA reports that the mothers' bodies are sometimes fed to the surviving puppy mill dogs. American Humane, another animal-welfare organization, reports that one puppy mill breeder fed dogs "the heads of slaughtered animals." There are puppy millers who breed hundreds and even thousands of puppies a year.

Puppies born in these operations are often shipped during infancy—at four weeks of age—in containers so tightly packed that suffocation is not uncommon; they are frequently poorly nourished and rarely given appropriate veterinary care. It is estimated that about a half-million puppy mill pups perish each year before they reach the pet store. Forget about such niceties as socialization and breeding away from hereditary disease. A May 1990 study by the California Assembly concluded that forty-eight percent of the puppies sold in the state's pet stores were ill or carrying disease at the time they were purchased. The study also found that puppies imported from puppy mills outside California were three times more likely to have problems than puppies raised locally.

Critics charge that AKC winks at puppy mills because of the big money it makes from them, money that goes toward funding the glamorous dog shows that lend AKC its panache. The organization's bread and butter comes from registering dogs, $7 for individuals, $15 for litters. ("You send AKC money, they send you a piece of paper with a number on it," Herm David told me. "They have an infinite supply of numbers. It's a great business to be in.") In 1990 AKC grossed $25 million, with more than 73 percent of that flowing from registrations. The *Atlantic* reported that, conservatively, puppy mill dogs accounted for twenty percent of AKC registrations in 1988. Most estimates run higher. A July 19, 1987 *Parade* magazine investigative report estimated that between a third and a half of all dogs registered by AKC are mass-produced. A July 16, 1991 *Washington Post* story reported, "About half of the 12 million to 15 million dogs estimated to be registered with the AKC are commercially bred."

By now this is a tired old controversy. In her 1976 book *The Pet Profiteers* (published by Quadrangle, the *New York Times's* book-publishing arm), Lee Edwards Benning reported that as of April 1975 just two puppy millers—one bred at least 1,335 puppies, the other, 3,500—produced north of half a million dollars worth of pups. Critics insist that AKC could crack down on puppy millers overnight by enforcing humane breeding practices as a prerequisite of registration. That puppy mills have been such an enduring black eye for AKC raises serious questions in the minds of AKC's critics about how reformable the organization is.

GENERAL IMPOTENCE

AKC bills itself as "a non-profit organization devoted to the advancement of . . . and the health and welfare of . . . purebred dogs." Perhaps nothing so indicates organizational waywardness, then, as the chronic ailments of the purebred dogs whose welfare AKC pledges to advance. Genetic disease experts say that in a fairly short time AKC could substantially purge its breeds of the most troubling hereditary diseases. All it would take would be to make testing clear of the diseases a condition of AKC registration. That is exactly how the International Sheep Dog Society contained the plague of blinding pro-

THREE: THE DOG TRIBES

gressive retinal atrophy (PRA) in the Border Collie, says Donald McCaig. But the collective body that is AKC—the breed club members who elect the delegates who elect the board of directors who hire the executives—won't do that. Why? The simple answer seems to be that AKC's culture values looks over health. Inevitably, however, it's more complicated than that.

Let's use the faithful Collie as our lab specimen again. "It is very frustrating to learn from a qualified, well-trained veterinary ophthalmologist, who heads up a major canine ophthalmology clinic in a large vet school in the midwestern part of this country, that 90 percent of the Collies seen in their clinic have some degree of defect and problem with the eye," writes Dr. R. F. Greathouse, chairman of the health policy committee of the Collie Club of America. "The veterinarians all know it throughout the country. It is not localized to one area, one kennel, or one breeding program."

In 1990 AKC registered 17,337 Collie puppies and 5,868 Collie litters. At $7 per individual registration and $15 per litter registered, that translates into $209,379 in revenue for AKC. Say the eye disease we're talking about is collie eye anomaly. In the bible of the field, *Inherited Eye Diseases in Purebred Dogs*, Dr. Lionel F. Rubin estimates that this hereditary condition may affect ninety percent of the United States Collie breed; it is seen in six variations ranging from mild impairment to total blindness. Eliminate ninety percent of AKC's 1990 Collie registrations and you've adjusted the organization's revenue downward by $188,441. And that is the result of screening just one genetic disease of more than 300 known in just one of the 135 recognized AKC breeds. Carmelo Battaglia, president of the German Shepherd Dog Club of America and an AKC delegate, doubts that AKC will make genetic health a prerequisite of registration anytime soon. "Eighty percent of their income is derived from registrations. Given the genetic conditions of a lot of breeds today, if you were to place these [health] kinds of conditions on registration you would economically cause disaster."

Do you see why veteran breeders like John C. Cargill worry about the possible extinction of purebred dogs? Obviously something has to give: either the culture which produces sickly dogs or the dogs themselves. So far it's the dogs that are giving.

In the face of such powerful conflicting forces, what should the organization do? Canine geneticist W. Jean Dodds suggests that AKC must either change or die. Dog lovers, she hopes, aren't going to stand by and watch their companions go the way of the passenger pigeon because of AKC inaction.

THE MONEY THING

In fairness to AKC it must be remembered that dog business in this country is big business—a $7-billion-a-year industry. If there is a whiff of corruption about it no one should be surprised. Whatever AKC's shortcomings, it can't be held solely responsible for the plight of America's dogs. Clearly, if the organization ceased to exist tomorrow, or if AKC were to completely revise many of its policies, those who most ruthlessly exploit dogs would find a way to continue to do so. Nevertheless, because much of the nation's dog business revolves around purebred animals with AKC credentials, a heavy burden of responsibility falls on the organization's shoulders. As New York dog trainer Robin Kovary says, "AKC may not be able to be a perfect policeman, but they can certainly make life more miserable than they are for irresponsible breeders, particularly puppy millers. Some breeders remind me of the government; we're finding out that they are up to things we didn't know about."

DOG PERFORMANCE

"Most people don't want a functioning dog," trainer Susan Bulanda told me. "They want a companion."

But plenty of people do want dogs that keep alive the instincts and working abilities for which they were originally bred. Sporting dog owners have reached an unspoken accord with AKC. They simply accept that English Setters, Irish Setters, English Springer Spaniels, Labrador Retrievers, Golden Retrievers, etc., come in two AKC models: field and show. Field types won't win you any ribbons in the ring. Show types will get you laughed off a field trial course.

Other performance dog enthusiasts, however, consider AKC registration the kiss of death. "People are astonished when they learn that our Alaska Huskies aren't AKC registered," famous sled dog racer Susan Butcher told *Outdoor Life* editor Larry Mueller in the magazine's February 1991 issue. "They act like it's some kind of disease! But if our dogs were AKC registered, they would soon have hip dysplasia, maybe hereditary blindness like the Siberians, and worst of all they'd lose their brains because some breeders would select for show qualities over ability."

As this book was going to press, a minority faction of the Border Collie People had approached AKC for recognition. Intertribal warfare flared instantly as an opposing alliance of Border Collie People sprang up. Representatives of the resistance included the North American Sheepdog Society, the American Border Collie Association, the United States Border Collie Club, the International Border Collie Registry, the Border Collie Club of America, and the U.S. Border Collie Handler's Association. The alliance also included such distinguished Friends of the Border Collie as authors Vicki Hearne (*Adam's Task*) and Donald McCaig (*Nop's Trials* and *Eminent Dogs, Dangerous Men*), *Time* magazine editor-at-large Strobe Talbot, and Clint Rowe, the man who trained Mike, Border Collie star of the movie *Down and Out in Beverly Hills*. The coalition ran this ad in dog publications:

AKC: Hands Off the Border Collie!

We own Border Collies. Our dogs are companion dogs, obedience dogs and livestock herding dogs. For hundreds of years, Border Collies have been bred to a strict performance standard and today they're the soundest, most trainable dogs in the world.

The AKC wants to push them out of the Miscellaneous Class and into the show ring. They seek a conformation standard [appearance standard] for the breed.

We, and the officers of every single legitimate national, regional and state Border Collie association, reject conformation breeding. Too often, the show ring fattens the puppy mills and creates unsound dogs.

We will not permit the AKC to ruin our dogs.

When Border Collies start being bred for show, Donald McCaig told me from his Yucatec Farm in Williamsville, Virginia, "it generally takes about four generations before the herding ability is lost completely. Once it's gone, how in the world are you ever going to get it back? Think about it. It's sort of like trying to reconstitute a redwood."

McCaig has reason for his worries. "In Australia, it took show breeders just 20 years to breed out the working instincts so carefully implanted in the dog by hundreds of years of careful breeding," he wrote in the June/July 1991 issue of *Ranch Dog Trainer*. "Philip Hendry, the International Sheep Dog Society secretary, recently wrote me that just 15 years after going into the show ring in Britain 'the show ring Border Collie is as different to the working Border Collie as chalk and cheese.'"

When the *Washington Post* reported on the battle of the Border Collie, it quoted Randall Lockwood, Humane Society vice president for field services: "What you are seeing in the Border Collie protest is something that we're seeing in many other clubs. The AKC standards do not protect the health and quality of the animals, they only protect the financial interest of the breeders . . . many of whom are totally irresponsible."

Criticism of AKC can sound acrimonious, but often if you'll draw out even its toughest critics you'll hear an undertone of warmth. "We don't want to bring the AKC down," Herm David told me. "We just want to make an honest woman out of it. If you really want to know what drives me, it's the suffering the AKC process brings to millions of senior citizens, children, and families every year."

The AKC process, however, may be changing. Wayne Cavanaugh is AKC's vice president for communications. In a long interview, he gave me a point-by-point rebuttal of most of the above criticism. Nevertheless, Cavanaugh suggests that AKC is beginning to make the kinds of course corrections observers like Cargill and Dodds recommend.

Cavanaugh is particularly emphatic on the puppy mill issue, insisting that registration revenue from commercially bred dogs is not a significant source of income to AKC and never has been. The organization, he says, would gladly forfeit all earnings from puppy mills and is doing everything within its limited powers to get rid of them.

According to Cavanaugh, in 1990 only 8.46 percent of AKC's registration income came from puppies purchased in pet stores, the primary outlet for puppy mill dogs. Not twenty percent, or between a third and a half, or about half, as reported in the media. And not seventy percent, or eighty-six percent, or sixty-two percent, as various animal rights organizations have claimed in letter-writing campaigns. "No one has ever called here to ask for those statistics," he adds.

Cavanaugh says that since 1989 the club has been closing down puppy mills based on cruelty to animals convictions and plans to continue doing so; it's the best means at the club's disposal, he says, because the Federal Trade Commission, under terms of the Uniform Commercial Code (UCC), threatens AKC with restraint of trade litigation every time it meddles in puppy millers' affairs for any other reason. Cavanaugh complains that the UCC "defines dogs as chattel. They're not living things. They're toasters." But by going after puppy mills for animal cruelty, he says, AKC shut down 21 large-scale commercial breeding operations in the first six months of 1991 alone. The club has now installed a computer data base that scans 300 newspapers daily for leads on animal cruelty convictions. Convicted parties will "never again be able to sell, trade, own, or transfer AKC-registered dogs," says Cavanaugh. Meanwhile, AKC has begun routinely inspecting breeders who register more than ten litters per year, "hoping that we'll find records violations that we can suspend privileges on."

With regard to cosmetic surgery, Cavanaugh insists that AKC's policy is cut and dried. "We find cosmetic surgery abhorrent and we'd love to find anybody who does it so we can convict them. . . . It's not easy to police, not easy to convict, and gets into very expensive legal situations. When we have proper evidence, people go." Cavanaugh told me he was not familiar with the Golden Retriever incident Herm David reported. He was able to track down information on the Airedale case, however. "The reason we couldn't give the handler life was because the incident didn't take place on show grounds, where our jurisdiction ends, and the surgery wasn't on a dog being exhibited at the show. The suspension was for six months, not three."

On the subject of genetic disease Cavanaugh clearly intimates that AKC is headed in a revolutionary direction—eventually making genetic health a "consideration" in AKC registration. To begin with, entry spaces for the certification of healthy hips and eyes by the Orthopedic Foundation for Animals (OFA) and Canine Eye Registration Foundation (CERF) "will be going on [AKC] registration papers and pedigrees very soon," perhaps as early as 1992. This step represents a major breakthrough in an organization which only a few years ago was reconciled to the registration of green, three-legged dogs.

Cavanaugh told me that down the road AKC might add additional, specific disease clearances on registration papers of particular breeds, perhaps even requiring such clearance for champions to receive their awards. Beyond that, Cavanaugh says, AKC could require sires and dams to be cleared before new puppies were registered.

But in order for such revolutionary changes to take place,

the shepherd that is AKC will have to herd its large and fractious flock to new ground. Neither Cavanaugh nor anyone else expects that to happen quickly. "The fancy, the delegates, will have to vote on this," says Cavanaugh. "We couldn't just sit up here [and mandate policy]. You have to unfold this thing over a long period of time . . . . You couldn't just say, 'Nineteen ninety-three, no dog with any disease can be registered,' any sooner than you could say in 1993 no human with any disease, inherited or noninherited, can have a driver's license. You can't require morality. It's got to work from the breed clubs, and it's got to work from the breeders doing their homework."

Emotions surrounding AKC are high, and many of the organization's observers will be skeptical of the extent to which Cavanaugh's remarks reflect consensus inside AKC. Still, they clearly signal a new direction which, if it pans out, should be welcome news to most dog lovers.

FOUR

Hereditary Problems In Purebred Dogs

Geneticists emphasize that all dogs are composed of two creatures—the animal you see and its genetic shadow. The trouble is that beautiful show-winning dogs and athletic field trial-winning dogs and cuter-'n-a button pet store puppies can be, and often are, shadowed by genetic time bombs. The bombs may not go off until the dogs have garnered laurels for, or won the hearts of, their owners. By that time, large broods of the dogs' handicapped offspring may have joined their own human families. Seeds of misery scattered on the wind.

How widespread is genetic disease in purebred dogs? John C. Cargill's review of 1987 AKC registrations revealed that eighty-six percent of the 2.4 million puppies eligible to be registered that year were from breeds with serious genetic defects. Through breeding that stresses looks over health, some breeds have degenerated into veritable blockbusters of hereditary illness. Veterinary geneticist W. Jean Dodds notes that by 1986–87 fully seventy percent of all Doberman Pinschers who were tested for von Willebrand's disease tested abnormal. Two years earlier sixty-three percent had, and a decade before that fifty-five percent of the breed tested abnormal for the disease. Dr. Dodds has also reported that a third of all the country's hemophiliac dogs are German Shepherds.

Hereditary illness affects all parts of the dog—skeleton, urinary tract, skin, heart, lungs, mouth, teeth, and endocrine and metabolic systems, too. Particularly widespread are eye diseases, which can lead to total blindness, and hip dysplasia, which can completely cripple victims. Dogs may be two to five years old before they are diagnosed with these maladies, and because of them each year many pets must be destroyed.

Genetic disease is now so common in purebred dogs, and spreading so rapidly, that there is no up-to-date book indexing the various afflictions to which the different breeds are prone. Moreover, publication of such a book is unlikely. "It would be out-of-date as soon as it came out," says Dr. John Kramer, a pathologist at Washington State University's school of veterinary medicine. The last widely distributed attempt at indexing hereditary disease, *Medical and Genetic Aspects of Purebred Dogs*, was published in 1983 and is now out of print. While it remains a text well regarded by veterinarians and veterinary researchers, it is generally thought to be something of an antique because of the dramatic spread of canine genetic disease.

Is there more genetic disease among purebred dogs today than in the past? Researchers like Dr. Kramer and Dr. Padgett of Michigan State University would like to say no. As scientists, they know there has always been genetic disease—it's just part of the living puzzle constantly being worked out by evolution. But Kramer and Padgett have to say yes, there is more genetic disease in purebred dogs today. This is because nature does not value form over function, as breeders do. Nature does not host the fancy dress balls of dogdom, the televised Westminster show in this country, Crufts in England. Nature does not award blue ribbons. It awards survival. Breeders in their zeal to produce winning dogs, or to mass-produce popular puppies, aren't screening genetic disease out of their stock and so are needlessly, and dangerously, concentrating it in their bloodlines.

Nobody has anything good to say about puppy mill breeders. And prestigious breeders scorn back-yard breeders. "But puppy mill dogs and back-yard breeder dogs don't get into the sacred bloodlines the way champion dogs do," says canine genetics authority Padgett. "We have matador [stud] dogs that produce up to 500 dogs. If those champion dogs carry genetic disease—as many do—it can spread far and rapidly."

W. Jean Dodds observes that the all-time top-producing German Shepherd stud was a hemophiliac. Every one of his daughters carried the disease, too.

Meanwhile, for reasons no one is sure of, the decade of the 1980s also saw a disturbing increase in the incidence of autoimmune thyroid disease among America's dogs. This was accompanied by a surge in von Willebrand's disease, a closely associated disorder that interferes with blood clotting and can cause untreated injured animals to bleed to death. We have these facts on the authority of a report in the August 1990 issue of the veterinary news magazine *DVM*. (See table 1 for a list of breeds now known to be affected.) The authors, Drs. W. Jean Dodds and Priscilla K. Stockner, implicated "genetic predisposition" as the primary culprit in the trend.

Immune-mediated diseases affect a variety of tissues and organs, particularly bone marrow, liver, adrenal gland, pancreas, skin, eyes, muscle, kidney, joints, bowel, and central nervous system. Investigators have established that, in addition to genetic predisposition, viral exposure, hormonal influence, and stress are primary causes of autoimmune thyroid disease. What remains a mystery, however, is why its incidence sharply climbed during the eighties, a period that saw an impressive collective effort by concerned breeders to eliminate von Willebrand's carriers from their stock. Because humans and cats have been similarly afflicted, researchers suspect common environmental or nutritional causes. (It is interesting to note that in the time it takes humans to produce 40 generations, dogs produce 400, leading some scientists to see in the dog "a genetic pilot experiment for the human race.")

One sickness commonly associated with autoimmune disease, infection by parvovirus, has been striking with such vengeance in the late eighties and early nineties as to stir worries

TABLE 1

Breeds Susceptible to Autoimmune Disease

Afghan Hound	Irish Water Spaniel
Airedale	Irish Wolfhound
Akita	Keeshond
American Cocker Spaniel	Kerry Blue Terrier
Australian Shepherd	Kuvasz
Basset Hound	Labrador Retriever
Beagle	Manchester Terrier
Belgian Sheepdogs	Mastiff
Boxer	Miniature Schnauzer
Briard	Newfoundland
Bulldog	Pembroke Welsh Corgi
Cairn Terrier	Pomeranian
Chow Chow	Poodle (especially Standard)
Collie (Bearded, too)	Rottweiler
Dachshund	Saluki
Doberman Pinscher	Samoyed
English Cocker Spaniel	Shar-Pei
English Setter	Scottish Terrier
English Springer Spaniel	Shetland Sheepdog
Fox Terrier	Shih Tzu
German Shepherd	Siberian Husky
Golden Retriever	Silky Terrier
Gordon Setter	Soft-Coated Wheaten Terrier
Great Dane	Vizsla
Irish Setter	Weimaraner

that a new strain had emerged. Subsequent investigation, however, revealed that much of the new parvo outbreak was confined to high-volume breeders and the pet stores carrying their stock. In these commercial settings, where diseased animals are often ceaselessly bred and retailed, the virus builds up to lethal concentrations that simply overwhelm current vaccines.

While there is a hereditary disease for virtually every part of the dog's anatomy, beyond any question one of the most emotional, controversial, and expensive dog diseases of modern times is canine hip dysplasia, commonly referred to as CHD. This is an ailment in which the ball and socket joints of the hips are poorly formed—dysplasia means bad development. Mildly dysplastic dogs may simply lose some tolerance for exercise. Severely affected animals often are crippled and must be put to sleep. The OFA certifies seven hip types: excellent, good, fair, borderline, mild, moderate, and severe.

CHD was first reported in 1935, but because it is a complex hereditary deformity caused by the interaction of many genes, it has proven maddeningly frustrating for breeders to control. Moreover, it resists the generalization that show dogs are more prone to it than field dogs. To illustrate, only about eight percent of English Cocker Spaniels examined by OFA suffer from the disease. The English Cocker is almost exclusively a show and pet dog now. Meanwhile, about forty-seven percent of the Boykin Spaniels examined proved dysplastic, and the Boykin is exclusively a sporting breed.

As Table 2 shows, canine hip dysplasia is much more of a problem for some breeds than others. For some breeds, in fact, it is the most common form of degenerative joint disease. OFA maintains that the only way to reduce the prevalence of hip dysplasia is to selectively breed for normal hips, and notes that scientists have repeatedly proven the effectiveness of doing this. OFA cites reports of dramatic reductions of CHD in Sweden and Germany through selective breeding.

Canine hip dysplasia is a good example of how invisible genetic time bombs can be and how arduous they can be to defuse. The only way to accurately diagnose CHD is by X-ray. OFA requires that dogs be at least 24 months old when X-rayed in order to qualify for an OFA breed registry number. The gen-

TABLE 2

Hip Dysplasia in Dog Breeds with Over One Hundred OFA Evaluations—January 1974–March 1989

BREED	NUMBER EVALUATED	PERCENT DYSPLASTIC
St. Bernard	1,027	47.4
Boykin Spaniel	287	46.7
Staffordshire Terrier	263	31.5
Newfoundland	3,735	31.4
Bullmastiff	752	31.1
Welsh Springer Spaniel	274	28.8
Bloodhound	959	28.3
Bernese Mountain Dog	1,726	28.0
Portuguese Water Dog	508	26.2
Chesapeake Bay Retriever	3,412	25.5
Kuvasz	447	24.8
English Setter	2,888	24.3
Chow Chow	154	24.2
Rottweiler	25,560	24.0
Golden Retriever	35,532	23.8
Gordon Setter	2,156	23.7
Norwegian Elkhound	1,615	23.6
Giant Schnauzer	1,160	23.2
Welsh Corgi (Pembroke)	943	22.8
Mastiff	926	22.6
Old English Sheepdog	6,363	22.5
German Shepherd Dog	24,827	21.9
Australian Cattle Dog	254	20.9
French Briard	445	20.4
Bouvier Des Flandres	2,087	20.2
Brittany	4,651	20.1
Curly Coated Retriever	233	20.1

(*continued*)

TABLE 2
(Continued)

BREED	NUMBER EVALUATED	PERCENT DYSPLASTIC
English Springer Spaniel	3,343	19.5
Shar-Pei	2,196	19.3
Irish Water Spaniel	290	19.2
Anatolian Shepherd	157	18.4
Akita	4,914	18.3
Black and Tan Coonhound	232	18.1
Border Collie	531	16.6
Poodle	4,288	16.3
Airedale Terrier	1,143	16.2
Cavalier King Charles Spaniel	203	15.8
Boxer	474	15.8
Shih Tzu	128	14.9
Labrador Retriever	32,483	14.8
Irish Setter	5,252	14.6
Komondor	429	14.2
Great Dane	3,241	14.0
Alaskan Malamute	5,889	13.8
Tibetan Mastiff	102	13.8
Samoyed	6,943	13.6
Puli	824	12.3
Weimaraner	2,749	12.0
American Water Spaniel	110	11.8
Standard Schnauzer	1,374	11.7
Great Pyrenees	1,620	10.4
Rhodesian Ridgeback	2,241	10.4
Vizsla	2,710	10.4
German Wirehaired Pointer	908	10.2
Bearded Collie	1,085	10.2

(continued)

TABLE 2

(Continued)

BREED	NUMBER EVALUATED	PERCENT DYSPLASTIC
English Pointer	222	9.5
Wirehaired Pointing Griffon	324	9.5
American Cocker Spaniel	1,710	9.3
Tibetan Terrier	727	9.1
Kerry Blue Terrier	253	9.1
Australian Shepherd Dog	4,267	8.4
Keeshond	1,373	8.4
Lhasa Apso	447	8.3
Bichon Frise	357	8.1
Doberman Pinscher	3,903	8.1
German Shorthaired Pointer	2,636	7.6
Belgian Malinois	159	7.5
English Cocker Spaniel	1,576	7.5
Dalmatian	843	6.8
Shetland Sheepdog	733	6.1
Soft-Coated Wheaten Terrier	1,503	6.0
Irish Wolfhound	502	6.0
Afghan Hound	3,361	5.6
Belgian Tervuren	1,195	5.4
Border Terrier	184	4.9
Flat Coated Retriever	913	4.4
Collie	661	4.1
Belgian Sheepdog	1,025	3.0
Saluki	137	2.9
Siberian Husky	7,092	2.7
Borzoi	394	2.4
Canaan	119	2.4

eral principles recommended by OFA for breeding away from CHD are:

1. Breed only normal dogs to normal dogs.
2. The normal dogs should come from normal parents and grandparents.
3. The normal dogs should have over seventy-five percent normal siblings.
4. A dog with excellent hips from a litter having more than twenty-five percent dysplastic pups is a worse breeding choice than a dog with fair hips from a litter experiencing less than twenty-five percent dysplasia.
5. Choose replacement dams that have better hips than their parents and the breed average.

Because sound hips are only one of the desirable qualities in a dog, dealing with hip dysplasia illustrates the challenge of fighting genetic disease and breeding balanced dogs at the same time. There are reports of many otherwise fine animals being eliminated from breeding stock, or even "knocked in the head"—as one veterinary researcher who has worked extensively with field trialers told me—just because their hips weren't perfect. The consensus of sources I talked to is that a puppy buyer would be safe in choosing a pup from parents with fair hips assuming they are exemplary in every other way.

Hereditary eye disease has become so widespread in purebred dogs that it is the source of nearly half the vision problems seen in canine ophthalmic practices, says Dr. Lionel F. Rubin in his *Inherited Eye Diseases in Purebred Dogs*. These conditions range from mild to serious, from easily treatable to untreatable.

For hereditary eye disease that can be treated—certain types of cataracts, for example—it isn't hard to spend $1000 or more at the vet's office. Some of the eye diseases we're talking about can be detected when puppies are a few weeks old. Others don't show up until years later, about the time a dog has become an obedience champion, or all-time champion family member.

Cataracts and progressive retinal atrophy (PRA) are two of the more serious maladies, but there are many others. Some breeds are relatively free of eye disease. The American Foxhound, for example, receives less than a one-column entry in Dr. Rubin's book. Others are plagued by it. The Cocker Spaniel, top dog in AKC registrations from 1982 to 1990, gets nearly ten pages. Collies, justifiably immortalized by Eric Knight's Lassie as one of the sweetest of all dog breeds, have nearly 12 pages of eye problems. In addition to Collie eye anomaly, previously mentioned, three forms of PRA are found in Collies, with the rod-cone dysplasia, or early onset type, causing night blindness in pups as young as six weeks. "Most [affected] dogs become functionally blind by eight months," reports Dr. Rubin.

Just as troubling, some breeds suffer from relatively few eye problems, but those affecting them can be severe. The Australian Cattle Dog, née Queensland Blue Heeler, is one of these. In this breed's case, "extensive multifocal problems exist," writes Dr. Rubin, and "there appears to be an unusually high incidence" of PRA both in U.S.- and Australian-bred animals. Table 3 provides a rough indication of the extent of eye problems in the nation's dogs.

Again, don't be too quick to point the finger at show breeders alone. Take the case of the English Springer Spaniel, a breed with seven pages of eye problems in Dr. Rubin's book, including two kinds of PRA, both untreatable and resulting in blindness. Focal retinal dysplasia (and associated defects) is a "potentially severe" eye disease that in England is estimated to affect sixteen percent of field trial dogs but only two percent of the show dog population. While some forms of inherited eye disease can be treated, the "cure" for them, like the cure for hip dysplasia, is breeding. In the case of PRA, for instance, neither affected animals nor littermates of affected sires or dams should be bred. Each littermate carries a sixty-seven percent likelihood of being a carrier. Progeny and siblings should be

TABLE 3
CERF Eye Problems For the Year 1989

BREED	NUMBER EVALUATED	PERCENT OF PROBLEMS (BY GENDER)		NUMBER OF CONDITIONS (BY GENDER)	
		M	F	M	F
Afghan Hound	115	30	34	20	30
Akita	297	16	20	21	51
Alaskan Malamute	125	30	21	22	24
Australian Cattle Dog	141	13	24	17	22
Australian Shepherd	1669	16	15	150	182
Basenji	214	72	69	122	119
Belgian Tervuren	146	30	31	24	35
Border Collie	242	33	28	55	51
Boston Terrier	124	12	27	10	33
Cavalier King Charles Spaniel	162	43	37	34	46
Chesapeake Bay Retriever	394	27	27	63	87
Cocker Spaniel (American)	4570	61	62	1419	2975
Collie (Rough or Smooth)	2953	78	75	1655	1605
Curly-Coated Retriever	104	55	42	43	29
English Cocker Spaniel	679	41	43	161	252
English Springer Spaniel	1442	23	21	202	210
Flat-Coated Retriever	153	45	33	40	36
German Shepherd	138	39	46	37	48
Golden Retriever	4311	36	32	698	1106

(*continued*)

TABLE 3

(Continued)

BREED	NUMBER EVALUATED	PERCENT OF PROBLEMS (BY GENDER)		NUMBER OF CONDITIONS (BY GENDER)	
		M	F	M	F
Irish Setter	112	31	30	24	22
Labrador Retriever	331	28	23	433	599
Miniature Schnauzer	796	19	18	85	119
Norwegian Elkhound	115	26	25	19	16
Old English Sheepdog	159	31	27	23	365
Poodle (Miniature)	562	45	27	128	126
Poodle (Standard)	433	22	27	54	86
Poodle (Toy)	704	26	29	80	175
Puli	127	34	24	25	21
Portuguese Water Dog	142	20	15	18	17
Rottweiler	401	40	35	102	104
Samoyed	728	39	34	161	204
Shetland Sheepdog	1576	24	27	221	309
Siberian Husky	2402	33	25	415	416
Soft-Coated Wheaten Terrier	375	26	15	50	43
Tibetan Terrier	233	20	19	24	33
Welsh Corgi (Pembroke)	404	33	34	69	105

NOTE: The above information is based on 1989 exams by the approximately 110 CERF ophthalmologists in the U.S. and Canada. Many breeds are not included in this table because too few exams were conducted to be meaningful. CERF is a not-for-profit organization established in 1974 to create a registry of purebred dogs free of genetic eye disease. More detailed information about hereditary canine eye disease is available from CERF by sending a donation to CERF, Purdue University, SCC-A, West Lafayette, IN 47907. CERF's phone number is (317) 494–8179.

examined ophthalmologically by a veterinarian certified by the Canine Eye Registration Foundation (CERF).

It is important to stress that neither the OFA examinations for hip dysplasia nor the CERF eye exams should be interpreted as definitive disease indexes. In both cases, the number of dogs examined in all breeds, and whose exams are filed with these health registries, are but a tiny percentage of the total. On the other hand, the relatively small number of these examinations may be a good index of breeder indifference to genetic screening.

One last piece of bad news (actually it's mixed news) about genetic disease: about ten new hereditary ailments are being discovered by researchers annually. This is not because of the advent of new diseases in dogs, according to Dr. Donald Patterson, professor of veterinary medicine and human genetics at the University of Pennsylvania. It's because increasingly sophisticated tools of molecular biology make detection of the diseases possible. Detection, of course, precedes the possibility of treatment.

The good news, according to Dr. Dodds, is that "the technology exists and it's affordable" for ending the plague of genetic disease. "We have a series now of what we call biochemical markers that track the genotype for a specific disease. In other words, you're not measuring the genes themselves, you're measuring the gene product. We can do specific tests from readily available fluids and tissues that allow accurate diagnosis."

Armed with such diagnoses, breeders can follow established breeding protocols to methodically purge their stock of hereditary ailments. Such genetic minesweeping isn't always an easy task, because modes of inheritance differ among the various diseases. Sometimes the process can take generations to accomplish, as with von Willebrand's disease. Nevertheless, breeders serious about combating genetic disease have an unprecedented array of tools and mounting knowledge at their disposal. A joint molecular genetics study funded by AKC, the

Morris Animal Foundation, and OFA was begun in 1990 with the goal of identifying the genes of some 400 diseases within the first five years of the study.

What could be of even greater importance, not just to breeders and veterinarians but to the dog-buying public as well, is a powerful new computer tool known as the Canine Genetic Disease Information System (CGDIS). The system is expected to be ready for distribution sometime in 1992. Also developed with AKC funding under the leadership of Dr. Patterson, it will make up-to-the-minute information on canine genetic disorders available to vets and breeders. According to Dr. Patterson, CGDIS may eventually make it possible for AKC to issue registration papers only to dogs certified free of certain genetic diseases. Whether, or how soon, AKC can muster the collective will to do so remains an open question.

Postscript

Physical and temperamental infirmities make dogs inconvenient to their owners, and in every city in America there are dog jails where the occupants have been incarcerated for that very crime—the crime of inconvenience. Under the convenience statute the canine race has essentially become a criminal class. Of the estimated 2000 dogs born an hour in America, only one in four ever enjoys a permanent home.

Maybe an abandoned dog's owners made an impulse buy at a mall pet store and later came to regret it. Maybe they didn't research the breed adequately, learning only as their pet completed puppyhood that it was too big, too active, too hungry, too furry, too ugly, too irritable, too noisy, too protective. Maybe the dog was sickly and needed health care the family couldn't afford—it's hard enough for families to care for their own health these days. Maybe the dog developed problem behaviors the family didn't know how to cope with. Or maybe, as shelter workers report happens too often, the family simply discovered its lifestyle didn't fit with owning a dog. (The Humane Society's Ann Joly told me that she stopped working in animal shelters because she could no longer stomach the needless sacrifice. "I saw too many wonderful, happy puppies killed because their owners didn't want them anymore.")

Whatever the circumstances, for dogs the crime of inconvenience is a serious one. It is most often punished by death. Not instant death, but death after a few days of imprisonment in a foul and fearful place. It has been experimentally demonstrated that dogs can smell the odor of fear in the urine of another dog that passed the same way long before, a warning to be vigilant for danger. Try to imagine the airborne graffiti of dog pounds.

If the nation's dog crisis has an epicenter—and it is a crisis if (a) you happen to be a dog, or (b) you're a human who loves them or is exposed to them or has children who are—then the nation's dog shelter system is it. The shame is that until the nation's dog problem gets straightened out, if it does, the two most innocent parties will suffer the most—dogs and children. Poorly bred dogs often make poor pets and get turned out of their homes. The "lucky" ones wind up in shelters. There they enjoy an average grace period of seven to ten days. If not adopted during that time—and most aren't—they are exterminated, either humanely by lethal injection, or economically by mass suffocation in a decompression chamber. An average of ten million dogs are held in the nation's shelters at any given time. This in a nation of 57 million dogs living in 35 million homes. Unlucky canine rejects are merely dumped or otherwise abandoned. They die of starvation, disease, beneath the wheels of vehicles. No one knows for sure how many of these there are—true strays are hard to capture—but estimates run in the many millions.

When people choose dogs carefully, responsibly, they do themselves and humanity's oldest and best animal friend a great favor. When they don't, they administer a mutual punishment and become accomplices in a sad betrayal of people and dogs.

FIVE

Where Good Dogs Come From

"A really companionable and indispensable dog is an accident of nature," E. B. White once wrote. "You can't get it by breeding for it, and you can't buy it with money. It just happens along."

White's opinion was expressed in 1940, 23 years before Clarence Pfaffenberger penned *The New Knowledge of Dog Behavior*. E. B. White might have changed his mind if he had read this loving and inspiring book. It chronicles a revolution in the breeding, selection, and training of dog guides for the blind, the most "companionable and indispensable" dogs of all. When Pfaffenberger and his colleagues first measured the training success of dog guides in 1945 and 1946, only eight percent of the candidates ultimately made the grade. By the time his book was published, and his revolutionary methods were firmly instituted, the average success ratio had rocketed to between ninety percent and ninety-five percent. In one year alone—between October 1956 and October 1957—Pfaffenberger and company raised nine litters in which every puppy surviving to adulthood became a dog guide.

Dog guides are selected not just because they are intelligent and trainable, but because they possess responsibility—the will and the judgment to care for their humans. The implication of the dog guide breakthrough is that if good breeding, selection, and training can produce dogs capable of the most exacting performance, the same methods ought to be able to produce wonderful family dogs.

But whoever coined the old Latin caution *caveat emptor*—let the buyer beware—might easily have had puppy buying in the late twentieth century in mind. Your chances of winding up with a mentally and physically sound dog, one capable of providing you and your family with the friendship that has brought humans and dogs together for millennia, will dramatically increase if you can accept this basic premise: you're on your own when you set out to find a good dog. You must be clear about what you're looking for. And you must be prepared to do your own homework.

It is tempting to say that good dogs come from good breeders. Or that good dogs come from good parent dogs. But I think you'll be better off accepting a different proposition: good dogs come from your own decisions.

There are breeders who are more yentl, more matchmaker, than dog breeder. Like the Pomeranian enthusiast I was told of who breeds dogs slightly larger than the standard because she feels extreme miniaturization results in too much nervousness. Once a year this breeder contacts every person she ever sold a dog to just to see how things are going. But there are also dog breeders who might as well be dealing in street drugs for all the compassion they bring to their craft.

These are the best of times and the worst of times for finding a good dog to live with. The best of times because there is more behavioral and biological understanding than ever before about how to make life with a dog wonderful. The worst of times because of the epidemics and moral failure already discussed. Make the right decisions and you'll deal with the right kinds of breeders and find yourself in good company. Make the wrong decisions and you can expect to be dealing with dog breeders who could give a straw if the puppy they sell you lives to adulthood, costs you multiple paychecks in vet bills, or inherits a disposition ill-suited for human companionship. Actually, I think it's possible that you could even find yourself dealing with—how shall I say?—more colorful individuals than that. In the course of researching this book I had specific puppy mill operations described to me that caused me to shudder and gave me visions of characters with whom I wouldn't want my family to come in contact—at least not without a good Irish Terrier around.

The search for a good dog today can be looked on as an ordeal. Or it can be seen as an odyssey. Guess which perspective I recommend? Whatever you do, keep the faith. At this very moment the good dog you are looking for is waiting for you. Maybe she's behind bars at one of the nation's animal shelters. Maybe he's rolling in the grass at the home of a loving breeder. Search in the proper way and you'll find the dog you're looking for.

But before you begin your search you should be absolutely straight about something. Should you even own a dog? Volumes have been written and spoken about this. I would summarize what I have read and been told this way: look into your heart. It will tell you that if there is no space in your life for a dog, if a dog's life with you will be mostly unrelieved solitary confinement, if you will not train your dog, if the *essence* of a dog is irritating instead of pleasing to you, if you want a dog only as a protective noisemaker or as a banner of the ego, if a voice whispers to you that should things not work out you can always take the dog to the pound, you shouldn't have a dog. You don't need anyone to tell you these things. Let your conscience be your guide.

The second thing you want to be clear about is whether to get a puppy or an adult dog. There are millions of excellent reasons for adopting an adult dog as opposed to a puppy. At any given moment you'll find many of these reasons, more than will ever be discovered by loving homes, passing through the animal shelters of the land. Hollywood animal trainers are great patrons of these places; many of the most beguiling dogs you see in films and on TV are rescued animals. Dogs trained for the hearing-impaired are almost exclusively rescued mixed breeds. Oftentimes breeders, show people, and trial competitors will have wonderful adult dogs which, for one reason or another, they want to find good homes for. A healthy, well-socialized adult—of which there is no short supply—will spare you the considerable inconvenience of puppyhood. Particularly for busy people, this can be a great reason for getting a grown dog.

On the other hand there is much to recommend raising a puppy. With patience and the commitment to doing it right, you can produce not only a well-mannered pet but a companion deeply bonded to you in understanding.

The Three Steps of Dog Selection

Think of finding a good dog as the result of correctly answering three questions:

1. Which breed of dog is best for you?
2. Which breeder should you buy from?
3. Which individual puppy should you select?

Conventional wisdom would have you begin by deciding on breed. Obviously, there is something to be said for this. It makes no sense to choose a type of dog that is incompatible with your lifestyle, as this guarantees the suffering of at least two parties. Keep in mind, however, that the American Kennel Club currently registers 135 breeds of dogs and recognizes 153 breeds and varieties; worldwide there may be as many as 600, give or take a few. And, of course, an infinite number of mixed breeds exist whose jazz composition of genes can yield wonderful animals with the proverbial health of a horse. The point is, if it's an overall experience of companionship and dependability you're looking for, there are probably several breeds you'll want to consider. My recommendation is that you do a preliminary review of breed literature (which we'll discuss shortly), investigate several breeds simultaneously, then buy from the best breeder you can find, irrespective of breed.

Here's what I mean. Let's say there are three dog breeds you zero in on, and you have a clear order of preference. After you've talked with people who own and have lived with the kinds of dogs you're considering, inspected several litters, and visited several breeders, let's say the breeder you're most impressed with specializes in your third-choice breed. I suggest you buy from that breeder. That's how important I think breeders are. The number of potentially good dogs in the world is roughly proportional to the number of good breeders. (I say "potentially good" because, unfortunately, breeding can't immunize dogs against poor ownership.) Of course there are happy accidents—keep in mind dogs appear to be at least as genetically varied as humans—and sometimes dog marriages of convenience produce stout and congenial offspring. But why take a chance? As long as you are considering only breeds that are basically appropriate for you, you want the best dog you can get. A beautifully bred representative of breed C, one whose parents and grandparents are known for their love of humans, iron constitutions, and equanimity, is better than a mediocre specimen of breeds A or B any day.

Choosing a Breeder

When you buy a puppy—any puppy from any breeder—you're vulnerable. You weren't with the dam before she was bred. You don't know that her welfare was carefully attended to, that she was in peak condition, well nourished, her immunization current, and that she was physically prepared for the stresses of pregnancy. You don't know that she was fed well while pregnant. You don't know that the litter received proper veterinary care, socialization, and nutrition. About all of this you must take the breeder's word. That's why you're vulnerable.

When you first lay eyes on a puppy, you see a baby, a creature for whom life is just beginning. But that appearance of new life is misleading. In fact what you are encountering is an individual with a lot of history already behind it. The puppy's past is prologue to the relationship you will have with your new companion. What kind of history was it? Did it begin with a responsible breeder's vision of balanced, sound puppies, and a clear understanding of how to bring them into the world? Or was it skewed by some preference of appearance or obsession with performance not in line with your own desires in a dog? And what was the beginning of life like for your puppy? Was it a slow awakening into the foul, unnatural world of a puppy farm? Was it an experience of benign, "innocent" neglect in the home of a back-yard breeder? Or was it the fortunate discovery of a world of warmth and security, followed by affectionate introduction to the human family? These are important things to know. An amateur breeder who advertises "home-raised puppies" is engaging in deceptive advertising if home is a place where the puppies languish in isolation. On the other hand, a professional breeder whose profession is a labor of love has much to offer. It's what breeders actually do, not what they say, that matters.

It is an article of faith in the dog community that good breeders aren't in it for the money. In fact, most conscientious breeders consider themselves lucky if they break even. What motivates them is a love of their dogs, a deep fascination with their breed's character, and a genuine desire to improve the breed and share its joys with others. Good breeders never have more dogs than they can give extensive individual attention and care to. (Be *very* suspicious if you see several litters on the ground at one time.) They invest enormous amounts of time in their dogs. Their dogs are often family members, and they are never mere units of production. Sometimes excellent breeders have only one litter a year or less. A breeder I know keeps several females, but none is bred more than twice in her lifetime. Good German Shepherds are hard to find, but one of the people I interviewed for this book knows where to go for one. She would go to the Polish woman in New York who, many years ago, gave her the best German Shepherd she had bred in a two-year period, just because she knew my source would know what to do with the dog. This breeder has been studying, exhibiting, breeding, and doing obedience trialing and tracking with German Shepherds since the end of World War II (since being released from a Nazi concentration camp, in fact). "She breeds for herself, every other year, or every third year. The puppies left over she sells—for a healthy price—or gives away. She would rather give a dog away to someone who will do something with it—the one she gave me became multi-titled, etc.—than sell one to the wrong person. She's the type who lines up puppy socializers before the litters are even born. You have to step in Clorox solution to go in [her house]."

The births of well-bred puppies are the result of untold hours of planning that include evaluating potential parent dogs, the study of pedigrees, and extensive discussions with other breeders and owners. Many, if not all, of the best breeders have a firm policy of never breeding their females to sires they aren't personally familiar with and about whose offspring they haven't had many good reports.

A shibboleth is a test—a password, a phrase, a formula, a custom—by which allies are distinguished. You need a shibboleth for identifying the kind of breeder you want to deal with. While AKC registers dogs, neither AKC nor anyone else registers good breeders. This may be one reason E. B. White found good dogs to be such accidental creatures.

In my naiveté I assumed that somewhere in this dog-loving land—where annual sums are spent on dog food alone that would fund the defense of small nations—directories of good breeders must surely exist. But they don't. Breeder lists, yes. Indexes of breeders carefully winnowing genetic disease and concentrating on agreeable temperament along with the classical virtues of their breed, no. At least not yet. Some breed clubs are more helpful than others in educating buyers about what to look for.[1] Many breed clubs are now launching vigorous breeder referral programs as a way of combating puppy mills.[2] By the time you read this you should be able to call AKC—(212) 696–8200—and obtain a 900 number to call for information about the various AKC breeds and referral to breeders in the breed clubs nearest you.

The problem with such aids is that they will guarantee your introduction to the dues-paying members of breed clubs, not all of whom are equal in their ability to produce sound dogs or their dedication to doing so. One nationally-known dog breeding expert advises, "Go to a competitive breeder. That breeder cannot afford to produce dogs that are sickly. Because, one, it injures their reputation as a breeder. And secondly because they don't want to produce dogs that go on [to perpetuate hereditary disease]." I wish that statement were true. Unfortunately, the evidence is overwhelming, as Drs. Padgett, Kramer, Greathouse, and so many others report, that the dog culture makes champions of the walking wounded—genetically defective animals that become canine versions of Typhoid Mary—all the time.

That's why you need your own shibboleth for identifying good breeders. It is essential for puppy buyers to possess such personal standards not only for their own welfare but for the welfare of dogs. As American Staffordshire Terrier breeder Cherie Graves told me, "Only you can keep bad breeders in business. The good breeders keep themselves in business.

[1]For example, the Golden Retriever Club of America (GRCA) offers a pamphlet called "Acquiring a Golden Retriever" for one dollar and a 75-page booklet entitled "An Introduction to the Golden Retriever" for five dollars. In addition, everyone who registers a Golden puppy with AKC receives one of the club's PALs ("Public Awareness Letter") highlighting hereditary health problems, breeding, breed activities, and how to get more information from GRCA.

[2]For example, 27 percent of all Soft-Coated Wheaten Terriers purchased in 1989 came from pet stores. In a year's time the Soft-Coated Wheaten Terrier Club of America slashed that number in half by urging the public to buy from club members.

They're not looking for a market. They're working a breeding program. They personally keep puppies from the litters they breed in order to enhance their own programs. The animals they sell as excess are going to be of higher quality. And don't think that money is the only qualification for getting a good dog. You can pay a thousand dollars for a bad dog as easily as you can for a good one."

Inevitably, all puppy buyers will have their own ideas of what constitutes the kind of breeder they wish to buy from. Here are a few of the traits that emerged in the course of my research as important to me.

The Good Breeder: A Sketch

MORALITY

I may sound like a preacher, but I believe the most important trait of a good breeder is good values. Good breeders care about placing good dogs in good homes. They may be passionate about canine competition, but winning isn't the most important thing to them. A commitment to breeding excellent dogs is, plus decency toward dogs and humans alike. As previously noted, the dog world will introduce you to some of the kindest people you'll ever want to meet. It will also expose you to competitive and insecure personalities who use dogs as ego crutches. In the case of the latter, you wouldn't want their stomachs; you wouldn't want their low self-esteem; you might not want their puppies either.

HELPFULNESS

A good breeder will help you prepare for your puppy, advising you on readying its new home and recommending feeding and training regimens. Once your new family member is moved in, the breeder will enjoy getting progress reports and will be only too happy to answer the inevitable questions you'll have.

WRITTEN GUARANTEES

Good breeders provide written guarantees against genetic disease. It is essential to get a guarantee on the hips and eyes of your pup, given the epidemics of hip dysplasia and various forms of progressive blindness among the nation's dogs. The guarantee entitles you to a refund of the price of the puppy or a replacement puppy should there be a problem. (One breeder I interviewed offers a comprehensive, lifetime guarantee on her dogs. "If there's ever a problem of any kind I want to know about it," she says. "I feel responsible for my dogs as long as they're on this earth.") The guarantee should also allow you to take your new puppy to your own vet within a certain period of time in order to have its good health independently confirmed before the sale is considered final.

Beyond the guarantee of your pup, you want to see copies of the Orthopedic Foundation for Animals (OFA) certificate on the hips of both parents, plus the Canine Eye Registration Foundation (CERF) certificate on the eyes of both parents. Do not take the breeder's word that the parent animals are so registered. Good breeders will not be troubled by your request. Indeed, it will identify you as a soulmate in the cause of canine health, exactly the kind of owner good breeders want their puppies to go to.

Be prepared for this experience: you are almost sure to run into "prominent" breeders who don't believe in having their dogs' hips and eyes checked, even if they are from seriously afflicted breeds. Both in my personal quest for a dog and in researching this book I had this experience again and again. For instance, there is a dog breed about which Michele Lowell says in *Your Purebred Puppy: A Buyer's Guide*, "He is susceptible to hip dysplasia and serious tumors." She urges: "Buy only from OFA-registered parents." A leading breeder of this breed, a person who sits on the national club's breed standard committee, told me she didn't have her animals OFA-certified because "I've never had any hip problems. If I ever start, I'll have my dogs checked." Even in the midst of a plague of canine hereditary disease, this ton-of-cure-is-worth-an-ounce-of-prevention attitude is still common. Be ready to decide for yourself if you find it acceptable.

OTHER CONDITIONS OF SALE

Responsible breeders are answering the distress call of America's dogs by trying to minimize inappropriate breeding. One way to do this is with "restricted transfers." These can involve a contract between the new owner and the breeder stipulating that the dog will not be bred until it is old enough to be tested for inherited disease and has been certified disease free. Some restricted transfers require that the animal be spayed or neutered at six months of age, with AKC papers not passing to the purchaser until this is done. You may not be interested in acquiring a pet under such conditions, but you can be sure that breeders imposing them are deeply committed to improving the quality of their breed.

HYGIENE AND HEALTH

Puppies are so amazingly vulnerable to a host of ills that their mortality rate before weaning is an astounding thirty percent. When they're just wee things, for instance—the first ten days or so of their lives—supplemental warmth is needed to keep the new fires of their small bodies in the 96–100 degree range. Failure to provide this one modest comfort is thought to claim more new pups than anything else. If food is left lying around, rodents you never see have a nasty habit of picking over it or urinating on it, lacing it with deadly leptospirosis. If food dishes aren't washed and scalded after every meal, if water bowls aren't cleaned similarly once a week, puppies can fall victim to algae or fungus poisoning.

These are only a few of the reasons why you should require sanitary conditions in any kennel or home you would buy a puppy from. Just because puppies survive long enough for would-be owners to cuddle and coo over them doesn't mean they're healthy. If you find puppies being housed in a dank basement or a dark, greasy garage, if you don't see hoses and cleaning supplies near the runs, if the place stinks, if the puppies have dirty ears (potential breeding grounds for mites, severe infestations of which can do so much damage that dogs must be destroyed), if their noses or eyes are runny, if the parent dogs don't appear to be in the pink, thank the breeder kindly and leave. You aren't likely to find the puppy you're looking for there.

Something the famous ad man Julian Koenig once said about advertising also applies to dog kennels. Said Koenig: "Here is the only test for good or bad advertising I know of. If you look at your advertisement and want to puke, the chances are it's a bad ad." A breeder who raises puppies in conditions that make you want to puke is probably a bad breeder. Under no circumstances buy from a breeder who won't let you inspect his or her premises. It goes without saying that if you buy a mail-order puppy you'll be taking a gamble that turns out badly for many thousands of people every year. It also goes without saying that you should never—not ever—buy a puppy from a pet store. Most of their stock comes from puppy mills, dogdom's "Black Holes of Calcutta."

Again, don't let the dog world prominence of the owner of either the dam or the sire cause you to abandon your shibboleth. I know of a breeding where a couple took their exceptional, imported dam to one of the top sires in North America. The male infected the female with mange. The dam's owners were unaware until their vet discovered that mother and litter were crawling with the pests, necessitating that all be treated with a toxic shampoo. I have since heard longtime experts on this particular breed remark that the handler of the sire is notorious for maintaining unkempt dogs.

SOCIALIZATION

This is discussed more extensively in chapter Six but it's worth a note here. Good breeders know that the best breeding in the world is wasted without proper socialization. This means that a breeder is responsible for a lot more than just the physical well-being of a litter. A brief telephone conversation on this topic should reveal sensitivity to the matters discussed here. Of course it is possible for puppies to be well socialized by breeders who don't know the first thing about canine behavioral development but who instinctively give their puppies the loving and handling they need. After all, that's what happened for thousands of years before science illuminated the dark corners of the canine mind. Still, you'll probably find that the kind of breeder you want has more than a nodding acquaintance with this subject.

CURIOSITY ABOUT YOU

If a breeder gives you the impression that he or she won't sell dogs to just anyone, don't be offended. Take heart instead. It's a good sign you're dealing with a breeder who views placing puppies as something closer to an adoption procedure than a commercial transaction. Good breeders will ask you why you're interested in their breed and if you're familiar with its drawbacks or special needs. They'll want to know that your lifestyle and living arrangements are basically compatible with the canine character in question. It will matter to such breeders whether you can provide for the emotional and physical well-being of the animal. Many dog authorities I spoke with flatly advise against buying from breeders who don't exercise this kind of discrimination.

Choosing A Breed

I once had a friend who grew up a cowboy. Born on a cattle ranch in southern Idaho, he worked on ranches in that state and Oregon until he was 30 years old. Then he hung up his spurs for a carpenter's hammer. His older brother kept ranching. My friend, knowing his brother used stock dogs, gave him an Old English Sheepdog puppy as a present. Big brother wasn't pleased. Said something like, "I can't have no show dog pet on this place. Take him back."

My friend assured his brother that the puppy was from working stock. Besides, he had no place to keep the pup himself as he would be away on a construction job for nearly a year. Now, both brothers had grown up with cattle dogs and understood them. The rancher said everyone knew the woolly dogs had been ruined and were no longer good for anything. My friend said something like, "Just give him a chance. If you don't want him by the time I come back, I'll take him."

Periodically my friend talked to his brother on the phone. Brother always said the same thing: "You better come get that dog." Finally my friend's job ended and he returned to the ranch. "Shall I take the dog with me?" he asked. "Might as well leave him," answered the brother. "Why's that?" "Well," said big brother, "he may turn out to be the best cow dog I ever had."

When the puppy started to mature he was constantly in the middle of wherever cattle were being worked. Cow business just came naturally to him, and he seemed to study the older working dogs. When the pup was about nine months old he was helping the brother and another dog move some cows from a long, narrow holding chute into a corral. The small herd broke into two groups, and just as the man and the older dog were pushing the first group through the corral gate "one mean old cow" turned and took the measure of the Sheepdog puppy. Deciding he wasn't much of a threat, she charged and led a small stampede right over the top of him. When the dust settled, there lying crumpled was what looked like a bloody carpet remnant. Just as the man went to pick up the body, the big rag rose to its feet, shook itself, bared its teeth, and stalked the fractious cattle like a wolf. The next thing you know the rebellious cows were dashing for the corral, the Sheepdog snapping at the rebel leader's heels.

HOW A DOG IS LIKE A RIVER

This story illustrates an important point about dogs and their breeds. No doubt the brother was right in his skepticism, because relatively few Old English Sheepdogs are bred for herding anymore. Still, the dogs were originally drovers, and my friend obviously got a pup from a line that kept old instincts alive.

A dog breed is like a river, varying wildly from place to place, never the same from one moment to the next. But unlike the River Jordan, the "River Dog" flows from the imaginations of men and women. What great dog breeding is all about is setting and maintaining type, and it takes true mastery to do this. Jack Windle of Dumfriesshire, Scotland, for instance, has produced English Cocker Spaniel hunting dogs so uniformly and arrestingly bright-spirited and athletic that they seem to be made with a cookie cutter. One would be mistaken to expect all English Cockers to be like Windle's dogs, just as one would be mistaken to expect all painted flowers to resemble Cézanne's.

Almost all domestic dogs performed useful chores at one time—the tiny Pomeranian was once a powerful sled dog—and as the River Dog flowed down through the ages their form generally followed their function. What vestiges of native character remain today depends upon where along the banks of the River Dog you find them. That's why some dog experts will tell you that breed descriptions should be taken more as folklore than fact. You'll generally find more important differences between individuals within breeds, they insist, than you'll find between the breeds themselves. Still, it has been established in laboratory testing that basic breed differences do exist in such characteristics as reactivity, trainability, and problem-solving ability. It is equally well known, however, that breeding can exaggerate or minimize these differences, which is why I consider breeding to be more important to the average pet owner than breed type.

The America Kennel Club recognizes seven general classifications, or groups, of purebred dogs: the Sporting Breeds, Non-Sporting Breeds, Working Breeds, Herding Breeds, Hounds, Terriers, and Toys. Some books about dog breeds give such romantic descriptions as to read like fairy tales. Breed descriptions in other books are downright laughable in their glowing generalizations. And, of course, many enthusiasts will paint their favorite breed in only the rosiest of hues.

Once you get beyond the romance of a breed's past you're left with just three considerations: physical characteristics, behavior, and health. Almost any breed book is adequate for supplying information about the first, but personal detective work is needed to inform yourself adequately about the second two. Most of the experienced dog people I spoke with seem to agree that within very broad parameters it is possible to describe basic breed behavior characteristics. It's just that you should never be lulled into believing that an Airedale is an Airedale is an Airedale. In reality, there are Airedales and then there are Airedales.

The point is, you cannot buy an English Cocker Spaniel in the same way you can buy a Chevrolet. You can buy Jack Windle's interpretation of the breed. Or you can buy someone else's. Generic dogs simply do not exist. That's why your search for a breed is really a search for a breeder who is after the same expression of the breed as you are. I know a Rott-weiler, a Doberman, an Akita and a Miniature Schnauzer that are extremely sweet-natured animals. They are infinitely more amiable and trustworthy than a yellow Lab of my acquaintance. (The Rottweiler, by the way, was adopted as an adult. The Dobe was rescued, also as an adult, from an animal shelter.) Similarly, Golden Retrievers are justly famous for being superb family dogs. Yet Dr. Padgett cites reports that rank them among the nation's top biters. England threatened to exterminate more than 10,000 Pit Bulls and other fighting breeds after a child was mauled; in this country a similar hysteria against Pit Bulls is never far from the surface. Here is an excerpt from a letter written to me by Bill Reynolds of Republic, Washington, a man who has owned many breeds. He is talking about his "little buckskin Pit Bull bitch."

To make a long story short she was a sweetheart, smart and not a mean hair. Believe it or not I even hunted blue grouse with her. She was with me most every day in the woods as I was a log buyer and operations supervisor. I still have clear pictures in my mind of her encounters with bears, badgers, etc.; that ramrod stiff tail and dead serious look instead of the usual happy bulldog expression she normally had. I lost her in March of '90 when I had my wife let her out to chase off a raccoon that was on the porch, down the lane to the highway where she was struck.

An attempt at quantifying breed personalities, and an interesting alternative to the heroic and vague schools of dog literature, is *The Perfect Puppy*, by Drs. Benjamin L. and Lynette A. Hart. It examines statistically significant behavior differences among the fifty-six breeds most frequently registered by AKC in 1978. The authors asked forty-eight small animal veterinarians from across the U.S. and an equal number of national dog obedience judges to rank these breeds, on a scale of one to ten, on 13 behavior traits important in pet dogs. The traits are:

- Excitability
- General activity
- Snapping at children
- Excessive barking
- Playfulness
- Ease of obedience training
- Watchdog barking
- Aggression toward other dogs
- Dominance over owner
- Territorial defense
- Demand for affection
- Destructiveness
- Ease of housebreaking

These traits are clustered into seven general profile groups rating reactivity, trainability, and aggression.

Are the findings accurate? Not very, says an animal behaviorist who was asked to review *The Perfect Puppy* before it was published. He told me the variables surrounding the traits weren't adequately controlled and that it would be easy to find numerous exceptions. Even so, as a general indicator of what to expect in the various breeds and what traits to focus on in your own search, I consider this a useful book.

A good way to use it would be:

1. Rank the behavioral traits most important to you.
2. List the breeds that best meet your needs.
3. Narrow the breed list based on the criteria most important to you—temperament, size and feeding cost, exercise and grooming needs, etc.
4. Use this information to begin your search for the best breeder with the best parent dogs and happiest customers.

Regarding breed health, there are two basic steps you can take in trying to avoid purchasing a puppy suffering from the hereditary ailments common to its breed.

Contact breed clubs and locate the most scholarly, credible breed experts you can. (AKC is the most convenient source of breed club phone numbers and addresses, but other sources are mentioned later.) More often than not you'll find very knowledgeable people within your own telephone area code. Ask them what health problems to be on the lookout for and the names of breeders most consistently "breeding away" from them. It is advisable to get independent views from two or three such experts, more if you have the time, in order to compensate for bias and knowledge gaps.

Example of a Knowledge Gap

When I set out to purchase an English Springer Spaniel after Tugger's death, spaniel veterans assured me that hip dysplasia was a negligible problem in Springers. In truth, nearly one-fifth of the Springers examined by OFA have been found to be affected. This is not what I call negligible, especially since OFA findings are generally felt to understate actual incidence of the disease (because many X-rays of obviously dysplastic dogs are not forwarded to OFA for registration).

Example of Bias

When Seymour R. Roberts, a veterinarian and assistant clinical professor of ophthalmology at Stanford's School of Medicine, published a report in 1960 saying as many as thirty percent of Collies might be affected by Collie eye anomaly, "some irate breeders feared that exposure of the problem would adversely affect popularity of the breed," he wrote.

Talk to veterinarians. The vet clinics of America are where the rubber hits the road when it comes to canine disease. Contact vets in your area and ask if they treat physically and temperamentally splendid representatives of the breeds you're interested in. Then contact the owners of those dogs for the breeders' names. By the way, be sure to speak directly with the vet instead of the receptionist. Receptionists often just read from breeder lists, and those lists are easily contaminated with names of puppy millers.

Actually, there is one other thing you can do. Become gregarious. The moment you decide to get a Chinese Edible Dog (otherwise known as the Chinese Crested), or a Glen of Imaal Terrier, or Feathered Saluki, or a Poodle, or whatever, you'll start noticing them everywhere. Don't be shy. Go up and introduce yourself to the owner. Ask questions about the dog—if you've got an hour to spare. If you learn that the animal is exactly the kind you're looking for, track down the breeder and screen him or her with your shibboleth.

The Happiest Task: Choosing A Puppy

On the forty-ninth day of a puppy's life, if you connected it to an electroencephalograph, the machine would record the brainwaves of an adult dog. At this moment a puppy has an adult dog's intellectual capacity to process the experiences of the world. Yet its level of adult experience is zero. At precisely this intersection of mental competence and worldly innocence, the dog's response to certain events will mirror the deep genetic steerage of its character. This is the theory behind what is known by the cuddly acronym of PAT, for Puppy Aptitude Test.

PAT a puppy properly and you'll perceive its personality.

Puppy tests come in variations dating back to the 1930s. Jack and Wendy Volhard hybridized the earlier versions in producing PAT. PAT's premise is that there are no good or bad canine temperaments, only those suited or not suited for particular tasks. PAT is felt to be uniquely helpful in matching the personalities of dogs to prospective owners.

Some animal behaviorists contend that popular puppy tests have never been subjected to the kind of long-term follow-up studies needed to confirm how predictive of adult canine personality they really are. Even so, there is little doubt that dog behavior has a profound, if mysterious, genetic basis. If this weren't the case you would be able to gather sheep from the misty crags of Scotland with a Portuguese Water Dog as easily as with a Border Collie. Reality is that the Border Collie is *born* knowing the ways of sheep as no other dog in the world is. The shuttle of history has woven this arcane knowledge into its genes.

Nevertheless, even puppy testing's most staunch enthusiasts caution that the tests cannot predict grown personality with anything close to precision. Again, a dog's adult personality is shaped by a three-star constellation—breed, genes, experience. Experience exerts a powerful pull. Abuse, neglect, and inept handling pull many a dog from what could have been the orbit of a harmonious life. Similarly, skilled handling and upbringing can make a respectable canine citizen of a dog who might have grown into a domineering bully in less capable hands.

Compared to the rigors of finding a good breeder and a litter likely to be as free of genetic disease as you can reasonably hope, puppy testing is easy. Not to mention fun.

The Puppy Aptitude Test consists of taking the puppies one at a time to a nearby unfamiliar area and evaluating their willingness to:

- Come
- Follow
- Retrieve

Plus their response to being:

- Stroked
- Restrained

- Elevated
- Lightly pinched

In addition, their sound sensitivity and sight sensitivity are evaluated by, one, banging a pot with a metal spoon and, two, tying a towel to a line and jerking it in front of the puppy. Each pup's energy level is also scored.

The exercises measure a puppy's attraction to people (coming and following), willingness to be dominated (acceptance of restraint, stroking, and pinching), tolerance of situations—like veterinary examinations—over which it has no control (elevation), and focus and willingness to work for a human (retrieving). (On at least one occasion PAT may have also registered a male puppy's amorous inclinations. A young fellow who offered to breed the tester's towel lure precociously sired an accidental litter when he was only seven months old.)

A six-point scoring system is used to record the pup's responses, and each response is scored and interpreted separately.

A puppy scoring mostly *ones*, especially on the restraint and dominance tests, has aggressive tendencies. This puppy won't readily accept human leadership and will bite if challenged. Such a puppy is not good pet material, but is a fine sentry or guard dog candidate. *Ones* are strictly for expert handlers.

Pups who score mostly *twos* are dominant, self-confident animals. They can be provoked to bite, but under the tutelage of a good handler can be superb show, working, or competition dogs.

The puppy who earns mostly *threes* is an active, outgoing dog who needs to be in a home where it will get plenty of obedience training. This puppy has great competitive potential and probably is too full of itself for beginning dog owners who aren't committed to early obedience training.

Fours are the scores of canine legends, dogs who will do anything to please. Easy to train, great with kids, the ideal pet for the average home. Puppies in this category usually lack the super self-confidence of top competition animals, but as eager pets they can't be beat. *Fours* posed for Norman Rockwell.

Puppies scoring mostly *fives* will grow into retiring, diffident creatures. They need a home that makes no greater demands on them than evenings spent listening to Bach or watching "Masterpiece Theatre." For quiet, elderly couples *fives* are just what the doctor ordered.

The French waiters of the canine world, that's what *sixes* are. Cool, independent introverts who will scarcely give you the time of day. These are the personality traits of many of the northern breeds used for sled dog work, and hounds—dogs, in other words, bred to do their own thing with a minimum of human intervention and coaxing.

For a more thorough discussion of puppy testing I recommend a richly informative booklet offered by the Volhards called *Puppy Personality Profile*; William Campbell's book *Behavior Problems in Dogs*; or *How to Raise a Puppy You Can Live With*, by Clarice Rutherford and David H. Neil. The latter, an excellent little book, has become such a classic since it first appeared in 1981 that many dog experts recommend it if you only want to read one book about raising and training a dog.

A question that occurs to some people is this: if every puppy buyer demanded well-bred, well-socialized dogs, would there be enough to go around? Taking the position a conservative economist might, the veteran breeder John C. Cargill has suggested that if breeders increased the supply of genetically screened dogs, buyers might increase their demand for them. What seems just as likely to me is that if dog owners demanded well-bred dogs there would be no shortage of breeders glad to oblige them.

A breeder I interviewed told me that dogs can see our auras. I don't know about that, but to be "chosen" by a dog is a wonderful feeling. "When you do that puppy test," this breeder told me, "if the results aren't clear, you want the puppy who is at your feet. You'll find the ones who are attracted to you are the ones you'll most easily be able to train." Makes sense to me.

I think choosing a puppy will always require a leap of faith. No matter how methodically you go about it, you still must wait to see how the stardust of your dog has been arranged. Who would want it otherwise?

Notes On The Canine Resistance

If, as I believe, those who breed unwell dogs for prize and profit make up the "lost dog tribes," and if their numbers are large and influential, as by all accounts they are, then what's a puppy buyer to do?

Answer: network with the good guys. Fortunately, it's easier than you might think.

The maquis was the name given to the French resistance during World War II. Named after Mediterranean shrub brush, they were tough, inventive guerilla fighters dedicated to a life-or-death cause. Maybe it's a touch melodramatic to compare those fighting for healthy, reliable dogs to the underground that fought the Nazis. But it's a comparison that occurs to me nonetheless. I think I like the resilient sense of adventure it implies.

You'll find the canine maquis in many guises. Cells of the maquis exist both inside and outside the formal ranks of the American Kennel Club. Inside AKC they are a voice advocating reform. Outside it they are not particularly interested in the politics or the fate of the organization—they merely act on their own to breed better dogs and place them in the good hands of owners who will appreciate them. Some AKC outsiders have informed me that it is a matter of supreme insignificance to them whether AKC should flourish or flounder. They note that just as the nation's horse breeders manage well enough without a single monopolistic registry, so could the country's dog breeders.

In every breed club you will find members of the maquis. A

breeder who publicly announces the breeding retirement of a genetically stricken champion is a maquis member in good standing, make no mistake. So is the breeder who vigorously screens for genetic disease. So are breeders who screen puppy buyers in order to do all in their power to settle good dogs in good homes.

The canine maquis, this loyal opposition, may be a minority at the moment. But it's a widely scattered minority whose members, masterful practitioners of the fine art of networking, can be found all over the country. You need only seek them out for more help in finding a good dog than you ever dreamed existed. Following are a few suggestions for doing so.

TWO WONDERFUL DIRECTORIES

The Canine Source Book, by Susan Bulanda, and the *Project Breed Directory*, published by the Network for Ani-males and Females, are, used properly, nothing short of survivors' guides for dog buyers.

The *Source Book* is probably the most comprehensive list of dog organizations and resources in print. Among its roughly 1500 listings you'll find not only every breed club and dog activity club imaginable, but general and specialty publications, registry organizations, health and safety organizations, supply catalogs, hotlines, veterinary medical colleges, support dogs for the handicapped, and fascinating general information about dogs. The author is a highly respected professional trainer and canine behaviorist who is active with search and rescue dogs. She wrote, and plans to regularly update, *The Canine Source Book* expressly for the purpose of helping dog lovers network with one another. This may be the single most valuable tool available for finding the dog you're looking for.

Project Breed Directory is an indispensable tool not only for those interested in adopting a dog from an animal shelter or breed rescue society but for puppy buyers, too. It contains nearly 300 pages of listings of the nation's various breed rescue groups, plus hype-free discussions of breed characteristics and health problems.

Many abandoned dogs become homeless not because of specific physical or insurmountable behavior problems, but because their original owners simply didn't adequately research the breed before buying. Good breed rescue organizations do temperament testing of the animals that come under their care and can be some of the best dog/people matchmakers around. A sled dog racer and breeder I interviewed told me that the best sled dog he ever owned was also the best pet he ever owned, and it came from a shelter. Breed rescue workers don't have the biases many other breed enthusiasts do, and because of that they can be an excellent source of information about hereditary diseases and behavior problems to be on the lookout for. Rescue workers also often know who the best, and worst, breeders in their area are and for that reason can be an important brain trust for puppy buyers.

A GREAT DOG BOOK SOURCE

If your local bookstore doesn't have any of the books mentioned in *The Puppy Report*, a convenient source for them is Direct Book Service, a mail-order company offering the nation's most extensive list of dog book titles. You can place an order, or request a free catalog, by calling a toll-free number: (800) 776–2665. The company is an excellent source of both introductory and detailed breed books, and hard-to-find but priceless titles on dog training. Some of the breed books offered are so unflinchingly candid they will, every now and then, dissuade a reader from getting a certain breed. And many of the training books the company carries are so good that reading just one of them could spell the difference between a successful and unsuccessful dog-owning experience.

TRAINING CLUBS

These organizations tend to reflect a cross section of local dog culture. Meaning you'll find both saints and sinners in their ranks. Responsible breeders can be well known in these circles because they typically impress upon their buyers the need for early puppy training and refer their clients to puppy training classes conducted by trainers they respect. Just look in the Yellow Pages under "Dog Training" or check with your veterinarian.

VETERINARIANS

Vets can be a source not only for information about good breeders but for advice regarding health problems of particular breeds. This is *not* true of all vets, however. If you can find a serious breeder of the breed you're interested in, get the name of the vet(s) he or she works most closely with. Such vets can have keen expertise in particular breeds and are an invaluable source of information about disease in those breeds as well as about the breeders most dedicated to producing healthy animals. But, because veterinary clinics sometimes have puppy mill breeders as clients, be sure to stress that this is not the puppy source you have in mind.

PET SUPPLY AND FEED STORES

The kind that sells leashes, bowls, and premium pet foods only. Not the kind that sells animals. The former can be a gold mine of information, and some even maintain breeder card files encompassing several surrounding states. Again, emphasize that you don't want puppy mill breeding.

FIELD TRIAL CLUBS

For the sporting breeds, whether you're looking for a dog to hunt with or compete with, you usually can't beat this fraternity/sorority as a source of inside information about where the best dogs are to be found. Trialers can also refer you to specialty publications and newsletters for additional sources of information.

NATIONAL AND LOCAL BREED CLUBS

These organizations will provide you with directories of their members. Remember, you must be prepared to screen breeders yourself. Again, the American Kennel Club or *The Canine Source Book* are convenient sources of national and local breed club addresses and phone numbers. You'll also find many national breed clubs listed in *Dog World* magazine, which is available at larger newsstands and in premium pet supply stores.

ADS IN NATIONAL MAGAZINES

Several dog magazines, including AKC's *Gazette*, *Dogs U.S.A.*, and *Dog World*, carry advertising sections. While many fine breeders use these sections, so do poor ones and puppy millers. In fact, I hate to think how many sad experiences result every year from the cleverly worded ad I saw run by one of the more notorious puppy millers a longtime breeder complained to me about. As one breeder told me, "An ad only proves that you can pay for the ad, not that you breed good dogs."

THE DELTA SOCIETY

As potential soulmates in the quest for a good dog, Delta Society members rank right up there with breed rescuers.

Delta Society is an organization dedicated to nurturing the human/animal bond. It was founded in 1977 by the late Dr. Michael J. McCulloch, a Portland, Oregon, psychiatrist who was interested in the way animals helped many of his patients. Eventually, Delta Society was taken under the wing of Linda Hines, original coordinator of the People-Pet Partnership at Washington State University, and her boss, Dr. Leo Bustad. Bustad, dean of the WSU vet school and one of the late twentieth century's most beloved advocates of pet ownership, had long been dedicated to the holistic aspects of pet ownership. Delta Society soon blossomed into an influential international organization.

Delta Society members are not necessarily dog breeders and often may not even be especially knowledgeable about the subject. But they form a powerful network and, because of their dedication, may be able to put you in touch with useful sources in your area. Linda Hines, now director of the organization, told me that, "People in our networks are very much aware of the need for sound animals." Members of one group in that network, Companion Animals for Independence, breed Corgies, Shetland Sheepdogs, Golden Retrievers and Labrador Retrievers with the highest temperament and health standards, says Hines. Occasionally they have puppies available for the general public. Delta Society's headquarters address is P.O. Box 1080, Renton, WA 98057–1080. Phone: (206) 226–7357.

SIX

Educating Puppy

A puppy coming into your home is like soft clay. When you raise a puppy you play Michelangelo with a living spirit.

Just before he died many years ago, a well-loved humanitarian in my town is reported to have said, "The last thing we learn about ourselves is our effect."

It occurs to me that any of us wishing to overcome such self-ignorance before St. Peter calls need only raise a dog. Dogs, and especially growing puppies, show us our effect from moment to moment. Just like any other mirror, sometimes they show us an image we like, sometimes not.

Even if you never intentionally teach your puppy a thing, the puppy will start learning the moment it joins your family. You had better *consciously* teach it if you want a good pet. Otherwise it will teach itself behaviors you won't like. This is guaranteed. Dogs are born knowing how to be dogs. They don't have inborn understanding of how to be acceptable members of a human pack. The best-bred dog in the world doesn't have a prayer of becoming a good human companion without proper tutoring.

In other words, one way or another your puppy is going to mirror your effect.

Like many professional trainers, Susan Bulanda is happy to advise people about how to track down a good dog. She tells them to be prepared to do what she does: spend a year—even more if need be—in the search. I, of all people, know how hard such advice is to follow. But impulse was never the friend of dog buyers, and never was it a worse ally than today. To bank the fires of your impatience I suggest you read a good book or two on dog training while you are searching.

As part of my penance for Tugger's death I took a long sojourn in the literature of dog training. What I discovered is that dog training books, of which there is no shortage, basically come in two types. One type endorses the use of physical force in varying degrees. The other doesn't.

Those who believe physical force is sometimes needed to train a dog—as did the frustrated drill instructor who presided over Tugger's introduction to obedience—subscribe to such methods as the alpha throw (flip the dog on its back to assert your dominance), the scruff shake (snatch the dog off its feet by the fur of its neck and growl your disapproval), and the use of the electronic shock collar (let the voltage meet the crime).

On the other hand, trainers who believe in reward-oriented training insist that punishing a dog is rarely necessary (and frequently counterproductive). There's a big difference, they say, between teaching a dog, or any animal, what you want and punishing it for what you don't. Proof of the effectiveness of positive reinforcement—Hollywood animal trainers call it "affection training"—is the spectacularly compliant behavior of certain trained animals who are too big to be dominated by force. Examples include the acrobatic killer whales and porpoises of marine parks, and the peaceable bull who ambles through the china shop in Merrill Lynch's TV commercial.

Something of a dog-training sea change appears to be under way. It is still all too possible to stumble into harsh training classes like the one Tugger and I experienced. And many popular books on training endorse physical intimidation. But an increasing number of the nation's leading dog trainers now renounce such methods. Dr. John Wright, chairman of the board of certification for the Animal Behavior Society, told me that his five-thousand-member organization would like to see punitive dog training methods abolished in favor of the kinds that stress positive reinforcement.

What is wrong with the widespread use of intimidation and physical punishment in dog training, say trainers like C. W. Meisterfeld, is that not only are these tactics destructive to an animal's spirit, they carry grave risks of creating dangerous canine psychotics. "Violence breeds violence," says Meisterfeld.

Wright agrees that dog training took a wrong turn when it began favoring the stick over the carrot. The danger with physically intimidating dogs, he says, is that doing so is based on the law of the fang. It signals the dog that canine, not human, etiquette applies. According to long-settled rules of the pack, you submit to whom you must, dominate those you can. Most dogs of any size can easily dominate small children. Plenty of dogs also have no trouble dominating adults.

Too, "punishment-training"—Dr. Ian Dunbar's phrase—really doesn't teach a dog what not to do. It just teaches what not to do when the owner's around, says veterinarian and trainer Dunbar. The owner, in the dog's eyes, becomes "The Punisher." For dogs punished into obedience, the moment of truth is the moment of discipline. They do what they're told because they fear the consequences if they don't. When dogs are rewarded into obedience, socialized into canine good citizenship, the moment of truth is all the time. They do as they're bid because they want to. There's no mistaking a dog trained with punishment for one trained with affection, just as there's no mistaking a person reared with a rod for one reared with love.

Training a companion dog, I have come to believe, is really pretty simple. Just start with a good, well-adjusted representative of a breed basically appropriate for you, understand how it learns, work a consistent daily training program, and don't make foolish mistakes like losing your temper. The secret is being well prepared long before your puppy comes home. If you wait on teaching yourself to train a puppy until the puppy is a wriggling, chewing, puddle-making fact at your feet, you will be committing a common and serious error. Fewer than half the dogs born in America ever celebrate their first birthdays, and one reason is that they develop behavior problems that earn them one-way trips to animal shelters.

In order to understand our effect on puppies it is essential to know a little about how puppies learn. There are key moments in a young dog's life—windows of opportunity, you might say—that appear to absolutely govern whether the dog will ever reach its potential. Familiarizing yourself with these key moments will help you be ready for them before your new friend arrives, or if you ever raise a litter yourself.

Snapshots of a Growing Puppy

PERIOD ONE: FIRST 20 DAYS

Nature has provided for dog babies to be born into something like an extended womb. For the first week of life outside the mother's body, most of their senses are in neutral. This reduces stress and helps them survive. They can't see, can't hear, don't feel much pain. New puppies need warmth to stay alive, but they don't even start to shiver until their second week; if it's too cold to live, Nature seems to figure there's nothing they can do about it. There is one sense that is firing even now, however. The puppy's 220 million red-brown olfactory cells (you and I have 5 million yellow ones) are already processing the fascinating damp molecules of scent. So during this time, when the pup worries about nothing, people gently handling it begin to smell like one of life's good things—like Mom's milk and warm siblings. Welcome to the world of humans, furry little one. Similarly, a pup not lovingly exposed to humans during its insulation from fear will never be able to associate people with low anxiety. For this pup, humans will always be somewhat intimidating giants.

TRANSITION: FROM 14 TO 25 DAYS

The puppy's other senses begin to connect as myelin coats its nerve endings. Now information starts to arrive about how the world looks, sounds, and feels. More complex learning starts to shape the dog's future behavior patterns.

PERIOD TWO: 21 TO 49 DAYS

This is a time of first impressions that profoundly influence what the dog "knows" about life. Introducing mild stress during the first five weeks—handling the pups, letting them experience such different floor surfaces as wood, concrete, dirt, and smooth gravel; gently pinching an ear one day, a toe the next; letting them hear a few minutes of slightly loud music; showing them flashlights blinking—has proven to produce confident, outgoing older dogs. Puppies socialized in this way are superior learners, and grow into better competitors.

At about four weeks, the age of individualism begins. From now on, personal attention will help give a pup the self-esteem that later produces a happy, eager-to-please dog. Five weeks is a good time for the pup to individually meet new people and children—briefly and under controlled circumstances. At six weeks it is disastrous for pups not to get individual attention. But don't rush to bring a new pup home at six weeks. This is also a critical time of maternal discipline and canine socialization. Clarence Pfaffenberger reports that pups removed from Mom's influence at six weeks have a tendency to overaggressiveness and lifelong nervousness. Similarly, if a puppy stays too long in the society of the litter/pack, its trainability is forever reduced. Seven weeks, exactly on the forty-ninth day, is commonly endorsed as the ideal time for a puppy to move in with its human family. Its brain and nervous system are mature. All that's missing is experience. (I should note that some terrier breeders have told me they take exception to this schedule for their breed. They feel that terriers make better-adjusted pets if they remain under Mother's discipline until the twelfth week. This assumes the pups receive extensive individual attention and careful daily human socialization during this time.)

PERIOD THREE: 49 TO 84 DAYS

From six to twelve weeks is considered the single most critical period of puppy socialization. Only during this brief time can puppies establish positive relationships with humans and other dogs. Canine authorities appear to be unanimous in this conclusion. This is also the time pups need exposure to many different environments, at least three a week if possible. (Don't take them to public parks or similar places where they could contract distemper, parvo, or any of the other killer diseases of puppyhood, though. Wait until your vet has pronounced immunity in effect from the puppy's vaccinations.) Pups need plenty of personal attention during this time to cement their concept of individual self-importance. Dogs who will be around children *must* be skillfully introduced to them at this time. Puppies need to be with their owners as much as possible now and should not be left alone for long periods. Don't fuss over them and touch them all the time—that will create "top dog" problems. Just let them be with you, and reinforce the kind of behavior you consider civil. This will properly induct the puppy into your family pack. The eighth week is considered a fear period so it's not a good time to introduce the puppy to the vet or other potentially traumatic experiences.

Touching proof of just how important this period is comes from the experience of training dog guides for the blind. Candidate puppies are carefully socialized and tested in the kennel, then (usually at twelve weeks) sent to 4-H homes where they are raised until a year old. They are then returned for formal training.

Pfaffenberger describes how 90 percent of the puppies who went to their 4-H families within a week after their preliminary socialization/testing went on to qualify as dog guides. Those who stayed in the kennel for more than a week but less than two before going with a family did almost, but not quite, as well. But only fifty-seven percent of the puppies left in the kennel for two to three weeks longer became dog guides. And of puppies left in the kennel more than three weeks after passing their tests only thirty percent could successfully complete the rigors of dog guide training.

Evidently, breaking off human socialization was behaviorally crippling for these animals. The lesson is inescapable: only if people serve dogs well during their socialization can dogs serve them well later. How's that for an echo of the Golden Rule?

SUBSEQUENT SOCIALIZATION AND THE POWER OF FIRST LESSONS: 3 TO 4 MONTHS

Life's events now start to accumulate. The puppy files them under categories of meaning first opened during the dawn of its ability to learn. A dog's first lessons stay with it throughout life, no matter how significant its later experiences might be. One of the foremost authorities on dog behavior, Dr. John Paul Scott, put it this way: "It is important to remember that, while previous learning may be altered by subsequent learning, subsequent learning will never obliterate previous learning."

About raising a puppy, trainers who stress finesse over force tend to give advice like this.

REMEMBER YOU'RE DEALING WITH A BABY

Not only must it learn everything about itself and its world, it must learn a curious language. Not dog language, not human language, but the strange, ancient communication of dogs and people. So be patient and kind. Keep in mind that all higher animals play when young. This play teaches them lessons not only of survival but of social harmony. So make training feel like play. Always strive to blur the distinction between the two. A dog who knows work as joy has a master of good effect.

DON'T GET TOUGH

Avoid harsh punishment like the plague it is to a puppy's spirit and confidence. Proper training involves clarification of the behavior wanted. Scolding before proper training has taken place is destructive. How would you like it if a new boss commanded, "Scialego pffbmahny etwologen," and then reprimanded you for your response? How do you think you would feel about working with that person—enthusiastic or nervous? Remember the lingering power of first lessons.

FOCUS

Before every play/training session with your pup, get clear about the youngster's limitations and the effect of pleasant reinforcement you want to have. Organize the session so that you and the lesson you're working on—sitting, coming—are the center of attention. Stop the session before the pup's attention wanders.

BE A PARTY ANIMAL

Puppy parties in which your pup gets to socialize with other (immunized) pups are a great way to promote positive canine relationships later in life. Parties in which friends and neighbors—*especially children*—come to your home and interact with the puppy in carefully orchestrated ways are enormously beneficial to adult dog behavior.

DON'T MAKE TIME YOUR ENEMY

This wonderfully vivid advice was given to me by Carmelo Battaglia. He means don't go too fast. Like overeager parents striving for super babies, some puppy owners push too hard, try to accomplish too much too soon. You can cause puppy burnout that way. On the other hand, if you won't spend ten minutes to thirty minutes a day shaping your canine clay, you're not being fair to the puppy or yourself. More than that may be too much. An excellent way to train is with minisessions of five seconds each, thirty times a day. "Sit. Good boy!!!!!!" If every minute of the training isn't fun for both of you, it isn't good training. Learn to recognize your puppy's smile.

BUILD CONFIDENCE

Take every opportunity to talk to your puppy in a pleasant, happy voice. "Shall we go to work?" I ask my dogs, and they perch at the top of the stairs waiting to accompany me to my basement office. "Goodnight," I say at bedtime, and they curl up in their spots in the kitchen. "Hungry?" I ask at mealtime, and they wait brightly at their bowls. (I combine meal service with sit/stay training, too.) Such routine communication not only helps to build understanding, but your voice tone gives the dog a sense of positive standing in your eyes. Will Steger, the adventurer whose sled dogs pulled him 4000 miles across Antarctica, sings to his dogs to build their confidence. I've tried it, and even though I have one of the world's worst voices my dogs seem to think I'm John Denver.

SEIZE THE DAY

Puppies grow fast. Compared to humans, they travel at light speed from infancy to adolescence to adulthood. The Italian psychiatrist Edward deBono, an expert on the mechanism of the mind, says the brain is a memory surface like a landscape. A landscape "remembers" where the rain has fallen by the course the water traces. The brain remembers experience by the tracery of firing neurons. Habits of mind are really the riverbeds of memory where the neurons have flowed. *Don't* wait until a puppy is six months old to begin puppy training; by that time Grand Canyons of mental/behavioral patterns may be forming.

MAKE YOURSELF THE BOSS—GENTLY

Lead, follow, or get out of the way. That is the native sentiment of dogs. Evolution schooled them in the survival value of order. They are born conservatives who loathe anarchy. Dogs become frustrated and are susceptible to a myriad of behavior problems when their owners don't establish themselves as leaders—or the alpha member of the domestic pack. But you needn't physically dominate a dog to be its boss, says obedience expert Terry Ryan. Why? Because dogs communicate through symbol and ritual. For example, leaders are dependable, so feeding your dog on a regular schedule demonstrates your leadership, says Ryan. Leaders eat first, so mixing your dog's food, setting it on the counter, then serving it when you've completed your own meal conveys the right image. Leaders are winners, so *never* play tug-of-war games. You can unspoil your dog by not always petting it when it nudges your hand. Having your dog sit to allow you to go through doors first subtly conveys the right message. *You* be the one to initiate and end game playing and put the dog toy away when you're done. Muzzle control is a dominant gesture you can practice by gently placing your hand over your dog's muzzle and praising it as you do. Grooming a dog is a loving expression of control. There is no more submissive gesture than for a dog to expose its belly. Dogs can be taught to do this gladly in exchange for a good belly rub.

THINK LIKE A DOG

My friend John Prideaux, with whom I train English Springer Spaniel field trial dogs, constantly asks himself, "What am I seeing?" Instead of interpreting every canine misstep as intentional disobedience and bellowing his disapproval, he ceaselessly evaluates why his dogs do what they do. Then he structures training solutions that make it natural for the dog to do, over and over again, what he wants. John is a tall man with a strong voice and the bearing of the Army officer he once was. But his dogs don't fear him. They adore him.

SEVEN

A Space in the Heart

As I write this Gus, the geriatric Cocker, is curled up in the corner of my office. He snores melodically as his old life drifts gracefully toward paradise. It is midway through a November morning, and outside it's dark and cold and damp. But I am bathed in warmth because Millie, the young Springer, is sitting beside me, head in my lap as I type, practicing the "spaniel gaze." At 16 months she's already got it down. The spaniel heart is warm. The soft spaniel eye brims with love. If ever the world's diplomats and arms negotiators learn the spaniel gaze there will be peace on earth.

At least the company of dogs brings a measure of peace to me. In a world that can be hard and mean I find it a source of comfort to have companions who don't know what a Scud missile is or what has befallen Magic Johnson; who smell the news in the wind, and find much of it favorable enough to produce a wag of the tail.

We can only speculate about how dogs and humans first got together. The savage canine ancestor was like a butler, dragging away bones and rancid meat from cave entrances where humans dwelt. He took to following these two-leggeds on the hunt, then led them with his superior nose and complementary ways of knowing the land. Finally he was adopted and bred for the purpose. That sort of thing.

But something else happened for which there is no archaeological record. In some people and some dogs there opened in the heart of each a space for the other.

There was a Cocker, Blackie. I remember his mannerly friendship. I was nine when he disappeared and I still recall the ache of it. Butch was a Boxer who would pull me all over the yard in a cardboard carton, never tiring, then wrestle with me 'til I dropped. He had angry scars over his ribs where a little retarded boy had stabbed him repeatedly with scissors. Butch was chained during the attack and couldn't get away. Still, he wouldn't bite the child to make him stop. Hank was a Cocker/Poodle mix who lived to retrieve anything thrown—balls, sticks, rocks. He died in the line of duty when a neighbor child didn't see a speeding car coming. Sally was an orange and white spaniel-like dog who adopted my helicopter platoon at Bien Hoa. During the Tet Offensive we were rocketed hard and Sally learned what bunkers are for. After that she always seemed to know when we were going to get hit and took herself to the bunkers early, suggesting we do the same. I don't think she was psychic. I think she smelled the news on the Vietnamese laborers who carried intelligence to those who launched the rockets. These are a few of the past tenants of my dog-space.

In 1923 a grieving Englishman wrote a letter about the loss of a dog to the venerable—sometimes eccentric—*English Shooting Times.* "People who know dogs as mere appendages, mere chattels kept for some ulterior reason, may wonder at and be inclined to scoff at human affection extended to a dog. But I do not hesitate to say that in denying themselves a dog's love they lose more than can be ever understood by individuals possessing such a narrow outlook."

It was with similar feelings that I set out to write *The Puppy Report.* Its purpose isn't to change anyone or to necessarily correct any of the sad problems which now plague dog ownership and dog breeding in our country. This book was written instead for those who have this strange cavity in the heart that needs the warmth of a dog. If the book helps one person fill it well, I will be glad for the effort that went into the writing.

Bibliography

Education for Puppy Educators

Talk to professional trainers of the "carrot" persuasion and they will recommend many books that exemplify the kinder, gentler approach to training puppies and dogs. You'll find dozens of titles in this category, but if you'll read just one your chances of having a happy dog-owning experience will improve dramatically. I pass along the four titles here not because they are considered definitive or the "best," but because each represents a valuable perspective for typical dog owners.

How to Raise a Puppy You Can Live With, by Clarice Rutherford and David H. Neil. Loveland, CO: Alpine Publications, 1981. For the average dog owner, this wonderful little book covers everything you need to know about how puppies grow and learn. It's an absolute gold mine of explanation and practical tips. Typical is the recommendation to keep hands off the pup as much as possible during training. Reason: a pup really isn't learning unless it's acting on its own. If it's constantly being jerked, shoved, and restrained, it's being controlled instead of experiencing the gratification and dignity of work. Although the authors do advocate discipline by scruff shake to curtail truly obnoxious behavior (they say it's much preferable to striking a dog), they are eloquent spokespersons for persuasive rather than punitive dog training.

How to Teach a New Dog Old Tricks, by Ian Dunbar, DVM. Oakland: James & Kenneth Publishers, 1991. This masterful and humorous book is actually the manual for Dr. Dunbar's justly famous Sirius Puppy Training Program. For those with a bit more curiosity about what makes dogs tick it is a fascinating read. With its great insight into the emotional needs of dogs, it is an excellent tool for dog owners who are serious about wanting a well-socialized animal. Before you even *think* about punishing your dog for misbehaving, urges Dunbar, figure out a way to reward it with at least ten times the intensity for behaving properly. The section on teaching bite prevention beginning with puppyhood should be required reading for all dog owners. (Dog ownership activists might be much more effective advocates if, instead of fighting breeding ordinances and the like, they endorsed such training for owners, perhaps even as a requirement of licensing pets.)

Don't Shoot The Dog!, by Karen Pryor. New York: Bantam, 1985. If you become passionate about positive dog training, this is a book you'll want to graduate to. The author is one of the pioneers of marine mammal training. Her subject is the fine art of behavior shaping, and you'll be doing yourself a huge favor by learning it. Shaping allows you to take the tiniest step your dog makes in the right direction and build it into super performance. With shaping, you can so deeply imbed desired behavior that dogs will reinforce themselves for engaging in it. The author points out how you can even use the technique to make a sweetheart out of a bossy old father-in-law, or a neat housekeeper of a messy teenager. You can also use the method on yourself to literally reshape yourself. Kay Guetzloff, one of the country's top obedience trainers and competitors, says the book changed her life to the extent that she actually lost 20 pounds just by following its tenets. *Don't Shoot The Dog!* is as useful to anyone who has a child to raise, an employee to motivate, an athlete to coach, or some extra pounds to shed as it is to one with a dog to train.

BIBLIOGRAPHY

Twelve-Step Problem Prevention Program For Puppies, by Robin Kovary. New York, 1990. This worthwhile, self-published manual is one professional trainer's personal answer to the most common problems of puppyhood. Its theme can be summed up in two words: plan ahead. It is based on Kovary's years of experience in helping owners correct the behavior problems that result when puppies aren't raised correctly. The advice this New York City trainer has on environmental socialization and how to avoid noise phobias is especially useful for urban dog owners.

(If you don't find at your neighborhood bookstore the titles mentioned here or those recommended to you by professional trainers, remember they are as close as Direct Book Service's 800 number.)

Index

INDEX

INDEX

INDEX